P9-CCH-389

OLD HOUSES

OLD HOUSES

PHOTOGRAPHY BY
STEVE GROSS AND SUSAN DALEY

TEXT BY HENRY WIENCEK

A NATIONAL TRUST FOR HISTORIC PRESERVATION BOOK

STEWART, TABORI & CHANG
NEW YORK

For Anne and Edith
—STEVE GROSS AND SUSAN DALEY

For my mother and father
—HENRY WIENCEK

Text copyright © 1991 Henry Wiencek
Photographs copyright © 1991 Steve Gross
Photography Art Direction by Susan Daley

Published in 1991 by
Stewart, Tabori & Chang, Inc.
575 Broadway, New York, New York 10012

Library of Congress Cataloging-in-Publication Data

Gross, Steve.
Old houses / photographs by Steve Gross and Susan Daley ; text by
Henry Wiencek.
p.   cm.
Includes bibliographical references.
ISBN 1-55670-184-5
1. Architecture, Domestic—United States.   2. Architecture,
Domestic—United States—Conservation and restoration.   3. Interior
decoration—United States.   I. Daley, Susan, 1953-
II. Wiencek, Henry.   III. Title.
NA7205.G764   1991
728'.0973—dc20   91-12615
CIP

Distributed in the U.S. by Workman Publishing,
708 Broadway, New York, New York 10003
Distributed in Canada by Canadian Manda Group,
P.O. Box 920 Station U, Toronto, Ontario M8Z 5P9
Distributed in all other territories by
Little, Brown and Company, International Division,
34 Beacon Street, Boston, Massachusetts 02108

Printed in Japan
10 9 8 7 6 5 4 3 2 1

Page 1: A painting by the owner, "Going for the Mail," in the pantry of Woodlands, in northeastern Georgia.
Page 2: A wicker high chair and an old icebox (in use until the 1940s, when the house was electrified) on the back porch at Woodlands.
Page 3: A crumbling adobe wall at Los Luceros in Alcalde, New Mexico. *Page 5:* The family tree at Blythewood in northeastern Georgia, traces back to 1153 A.D.
in England. *Page 6:* Delicate frescoes and faux-marble niches in the entrance hall at Coolmore in Tarboro, North Carolina. *Page 8:* Faux-wood wallpaper in the
dining room at Roseland in Natchez, Louisiana. *Page 9:* A detail of the living room at Blythewood in northeastern Georgia. *Page 10:* A collapsed chair leans
against a wall at Whitehall in Corydon, Pennsylvania. *Page 11:* The remains of a bird's nest lie in a bathroom sink at the Peaslee-Shelmandine House in Schoharie
County, New York. *Page 12:* A corner of the dining room at Barrington Hall in Roswell, Georgia. *Page 13:* Wallpaper lines the front stairway and halls of
the Peaslee-Shelmandine House in Schoharie County, New York. *Page 14:* Faded stenciling on the kitchen wall of the Peaslee-Shelmandine House in Schoharie
County, New York. *Page 15, left:* A fragile old dress in an upstairs window at the Peaslee-Shelmandine House; *center:* Curved lead pipes in the pantry at the
Skolfield-Whittier House, in Brunswick, Maine; *right:* Dilapidated shutters at the Peaslee-Shelmandine House. *Page 76:* Moss-covered verandah at Ashland/Belle
Helene, near Geismar, Louisiana. *Page 77, left:* Circular staircase with trompe l'oeil paneling at Coolmore in Tarboro, North Carolina; *center:* Abstract layers
of paint at an abandoned house in Opelika, Alabama; *right:* A detail of the kitchen at Barrington Hall in Roswell, Georgia. *Page 164:* An upstairs bedroom
at Los Luceros in Alcalde, New Mexico. *Page 165, left:* A window reveals the thick adobe walls at Los Luceros; *center:* An archway between a dining room and
living room at the Riordan House in Flagstaff, Arizona; *right:* A wooden staircase in a crumbling passageway at Los Luceros.
Page 240: Wild yellow roses across a window at Los Luceros in Alcalde, New Mexico.

ACKNOWLEDGMENTS

We'd first like to thank all the home owners who showed us so much generous hospitality and graciously allowed us into their homes to photograph.

We're also very grateful to Catherine Seiberling, Mills Lane, Bobby DeBlieux, and George Boan for their help in locating some of the houses that went into the book and for opening many doors for us.

Special thanks to Nancy Lindemeyer, editor of Victoria magazine, for her continued enthusiastic support of our project and her kind permission to use shots of the Gibson House.

Thanks also to everyone at Stewart, Tabori & Chang, who gave us the chance to realize this book and the freedom to explore the country to discover the dilapidated elegance of old houses.

And, finally, many thanks to our families and friends, who all helped in so many ways: A. D., Edith, Plum, Ernie, Nick, Tom Glauser, James Osterberg, Helen, Jack, the Kowalski family, Josie Fuller, L. Cohen, Amos and Mildred, and, of course, Celia, for the first camera.

STEVE GROSS AND SUSAN DALEY

I am very grateful for the kind hospitality I was shown by the house owners, without whose cooperation this book would not have been possible. They welcomed me into their homes, shared freely their private documents and memories, and then patiently endured numerous inquiring telephone calls. I am also grateful to the many curators and historians who shared their expertise and took the time to guide me through collections of personal papers and other documents. I thank Brian Hotchkiss for offering this project to me and Jane Colihan for providing invaluable advice and support at a critical stage. To my wife, Donna, a large thank-you for enduring my long absences and for her advice at the beginning, middle, and end of this project.

I also extend my deepest thanks to the following people, who were helpful in various ways in the preparation of this book: J. Winthrop Aldrich; Emma Beasley; George Boan; John Burrows; Paul Calloway; Tim Chester; John Copeland; Josephine Fuller; T. G. Futch; Althea Grob; Peter and Lucy Hairston; Armandine Handy; William and Douglas Hayward; Eric Jorgensen; Douglas Kent; Anne Hyde Logan; Delphina Mott; Neil Poese; Frederica Poett; Mary and Edmund Rhett; Catherine L. Seiberling; Ernest Shealy, Jr.; Betty Van Zant; Rudy Vom Saal; John C. Woodward.

These books, articles, and unpublished research reports were especially useful in the preparation of the text: Ruth W. Armstrong, The Chases of Cimarron; Helen Blumenschein, "Recuerdos—Early Days of the Blumenschein Family"; Hansi Durlach, and Stewart and Deborah Blumin, The Short Season of Sharon Springs; Edith Fox, "George Clarke of Hyde Hall"; Marilyn Hinkley, "The Skolfield-Whittier House and Its Occupants 1857–1925"; John Kollock, These Gentle Hills; Gustave E. Mueller, "The Chapman Hotel at North Blenheim," Schoharie County Historical Review, Fall–Winter 1981; A. Dibblee Poett, Rancho San Julian; Catherine L. Seiberling, "The Gibson House"; Walter Wagner, Inside the Golden Ghetto.

The private homes described in this book are not open to the public. The Aiken-Rhett House, owned by The Charleston Museum, is open daily for tours; admission is charged. Some of the rooms may be closed for stabilization. Ashland/Belle Helene, the Blumenschein House, Riordan House, and Skolfield-Whittier House are also open for tours on a regular basis. Tours of the Robinson House can be reserved by telephoning the Robinson Gardens. Other houses that are also open on a limited basis are the Ennis-Brown House, Gibson House, and Hyde Hall. The Chapman Hotel accepts guests and is open daily for meals.

HENRY WIENCEK

CONTENTS

INTRODUCTION

*W*E HAVE BEEN WORKING ON THIS *project about America's old houses for over five years. Our quest began in Charleston, South Carolina, when we happened upon an incredible old mansion in a dilapidated state. It sat in the middle of an old neighborhood, its piazzas and stately columns falling toward the street, its shutters faded and peeling, and its stucco walls cracked and pitted with the passage of time. We noticed a tiny sign that read,* RING BELL FOR TOUR.

Entering the house was like stepping into a time warp. We felt as though suddenly we were getting a real glimpse into the past. We used all the film we had with us that day, photographing rooms that had been sealed off for more than seventy years. Moving through the house from room to room, following the sunlight, we decided to use very long exposures in order to try to capture the imprints of the past lives we felt lingered there. Spiderwebs, dust, and ghostly presences guarded against the glare of the world outside. Later, upon seeing the film, we realized the house held a magical quality, and thus decided to share our vision.

Both of us have been fascinated with exploring and wandering through abandoned places since we were children. We like looking at the ruined walls of "haunted houses" and seeing pieces of wallpaper from the 1930s overlaying fragments of murals from the Victorian era. We are intrigued by the exposed lathing and plaster that were put over handmade bricks, which lie between original beams. Often these beams show the marks of the old axes that felled the trees, which once grew on the land where the houses still stand.

Like ancient pieces of pottery unearthed after centuries of repose—cracked, faded, and broken—these houses possess a beauty and truthfulness more real and valuable than any replica could ever be. The bones and skeletons of the beams and the walls tell the stories of how the houses came to be and who they are.

So, it was the lost house that we sought—the neglected, the sentimental, the things too frayed and worn to still use but too loved to just throw away. We traveled all over the country, mostly on old back roads and highways, for that is where we would find these treasures. Poverty and indifference were usually the conservators, protecting the places that had no discernible investment value. Sometimes groups of concerned citizens had adopted a house to keep it from becoming a housing development or a parking lot. But sometimes we met with dead ends; we had arrived too late.

We started meeting the last of America's oldest families, who were staying on as best they could and persevering despite hardship.

Instead of succumbing to the pressures of our modern age—by tearing their houses down, redecorating them, making unsightly renovations, or simply giving up—these people knew that the true value of their homes lay in their history, whether it mattered to anyone else or not. They, and the museum directors who have been entrusted with the care of some of the houses in this book, are keeping them much the way they were when the ancestral owners lived there; we hope that is the way they will remain.

These houses are shrines to the past, sacred spaces, in a way, yet at the same time they attest to the reality that the past is still very much a part of today.

So many people welcomed us into the houses, almost seeming at times as if they had been expecting us. They let us photograph to our heart's content, trusting us to move precious objects that had not been touched for many years. They let us peek behind closed doors and proudly showed us their family treasures, always sharing the memories surrounding each of them. We were very lucky to have found the houses that we did. And yet we can't forget the stories of all the great houses that are already gone. The one phrase we heard over and over wherever we went was, "You should have been here last year."

STEVE GROSS AND SUSAN DALEY

THE NORTHEAST

HYDE HALL
COOPERSTOWN, NEW YORK

ABOVE: *What was originally the billiards room was converted to a bedroom in the early 1900s. The shelves between the windows were added during that conversion. On the tilt-top tea table is a photograph of a painting of George Clarke, the builder's grandson.* OPPOSITE: *Some original paint, a robust shade of Prussian blue, survives in another bedroom at Hyde Hall. The sofa was made in the 1880s. Behind it is a golden quiver—it once supported drapery in the dining room. Other elements of the gilded dining room window garniture rest on the floor and the sofa.*

O n the northern shore of Otsego Lake in central New York, George Clarke built a "splendid and costly" mansion, a "princely establishment" where the owners and their guests enjoyed "gay, frolicsome times," in the words of one man who was present at some of the revels in the 1820s and 1830s. Constructed between 1817 and 1835, Hyde Hall would be the home of a succession of Clarkes until 1962. It is a large limestone building of forty-one rooms, with a plain, massively proportioned neoclassical façade and a four-columned Doric portico at the center. It was designed by Philip Hooker, the architect who had designed many of the finest buildings in Albany.

Born in France in 1768, Clarke came to the United States in 1789 to claim an inheritance of 56,000 acres of land in New York. The land had been acquired by his great-grandfather, a royal lieutenant governor of New York, who envisioned the development of a thriving industrial and agricultural economy in his rural domain. George Clarke inherited the vision as well as the land. After his initial visit to New York, business commitments brought him back to England for several years, but he returned for good in 1806

and established himself at Albany. Realizing that his holdings would best be managed if he lived closer to them, he began construction of Hyde Hall. In 1824 he inherited Jamaican sugar plantations from his grandmother, which provided the funds to make Hyde Hall a grand country seat.

The three formal rooms in the front—entrance hall, dining room, and drawing room—are massive in their size and proportions, no doubt calculated to awe the visitor. The ceilings of the three rooms are adorned with large plaster medallions; equally impressive is the drawing room frieze, embellished with thick vines that resemble, at first glance, a writhing snake. The walls of these rooms were sprinkled with sand containing quartz, so that flickering candlelight would create a twinkling effect, as if guests were surrounded by thousands of tiny stars. With eighteen-foot ceilings, the formal rooms are two stories high and contrast markedly with the much smaller rooms behind them, arranged around a central courtyard.

A traveling Briton remarked approvingly that Hyde Hall was like "the good English 'squire mansions'" of home. A Cooperstown attorney and judge named Levi Beardsley wrote that Clarke was "thoroughly English," sang English songs at the table, and "delighted to have his dinner got up in old English style, with the best of roast beef and mutton." The resolute Englishness of Clarke's house and his habits caused a certain uneasiness among his neighbors, and Clarke faced the general resentment against landlords whose holdings had survived the Revolution, even though he was fair, and often generous, in his dealings with tenants. One local writer declared that its "air of an English country-seat, with squire and tenantry, [was] transplanted to the soil of an alien democracy."

Beardsley professed to be dismayed by the wild life at Hyde Hall but continued to go to the Clarkes' parties. Heavy

ABOVE, TOP: *A table, decorated with incised chrysanthemums, and a pair of ottomans stand in a corridor. The postcards and letters on the table are reminders of the Clarkes' travels—many members of the family traveled to Europe and elsewhere. The red velvet of the ottomans has worn away, revealing the original covering of Belgian carpet, which matched the border of the carpet in the dining room.* ABOVE, BOTTOM: *This pair of bentwood chairs is not original to the house and their presence in it mystifies the family. They stand in a room where a water closet was installed in 1935.* OPPOSITE: *Huge triple windows illuminate the dining room, one of two enormous formal rooms at Hyde Hall. The empire furniture was made for the house in the 1820s.*

ABOVE: *This ground-floor corridor, leading from the stair hall, is lit by windows looking into the central courtyard. Hyde Hall's long corridors have a strangely claustrophobic atmosphere. In the early 1900s a local writer said that the mansion was at its best when it was crowded; a lone visitor senses an eeriness about the place.* RIGHT: *Part of a two-room guest suite in one of the oldest parts of the house, this room shows evidence of the settling of the rear wall: the limestone rubble wall below the window has separated from a brick pier, making a crack large enough to reach through. A superb gilt frame for a mirror is stored here, along with a folding chair with a seat of badly deteriorated Brussels carpet.*

drinking was the widespread custom in those days, and the Clarkes dispensed liquor freely. At one party Beardsley attended, some of the inebriated guests ran footraces in the dark, "but with no great credit to themselves as pedestrians." One of the company passed out on the threshold at the end of the evening, and the servants could not close the door. From the master's bedroom came the groggy order, "Drag him in and put him under the table," which they did.

The person who most enjoyed putting gossip about the Clarkes on paper was James Fenimore Cooper, the grandson of the famous writer. "Tradition says," he wrote in his *Legends and Traditions of a Northern County* in 1920, "that it had been a gay and somewhat wild life which had been lived there, and my mother has told me of the desperate

gaming indulged in." Cooper had been a friend of various Clarkes for fifty years and had frequently enjoyed their hospitality. Nonetheless, he relished telling the tales he had heard of them: "One [story] tells how, in the dead of night, the piano in the vast drawing room plays tirelessly; another of the underground passageway . . . to the family vault, through which the dead passed back and forth." He said that the ghost of the first George Clarke was regularly seen at night, walking about in a dressing gown. One night "as dark as the plague of Egypt," the ghost pulled the sheets off Cooper's bed while its occupant quaked in terror.

Oddly enough, Cooper's raciest pages of Hyde Hall stories involved his own great-aunt. Cooper reported that the beautiful Ann Cary Cooper, whose husband was the brother

ABOVE: *The dressing room on the first floor has a neoclassical chair rail of curly maple. The mirror, original to the house but undocumented, reflects a wooden ceiling installed around 1880, when the original, badly deteriorated ceiling was removed.*
LEFT: *This handsome blue table, with finely carved lion feet and a tapered octagonal pedestal, is one of the house's puzzles. No reference to it appears in the many invoices from George Clarke's furniture dealers. It was painted with a milk-based paint, a long-lasting type of paint widely used in the early nineteenth century. Well over a hundred years old, the paint of this table has not peeled or cracked. The table stands in an upstairs hall.*

ABOVE: *Severe dry rot forced the temporary removal of paneling below this window in the dining room, exposing the unfinished back of a limestone slab.* RIGHT: *A portrait of the second George Clarke to live at Hyde Hall hangs over a serving table in the dining room. The square white patch is the repair to a gouge in the wall made in the 1960s by state officials, who were trying to discover the exact composition of the wall.*
OPPOSITE: *Lilacs, gathered from the front yard, rest in the dining room on a butler's table made in the 1820s. The drawer was designed to hold wine bottles standing up. The room received its coat of distinctive red paint as a prank in 1883. The builder's grandson, who would take possession of the house a few years later, went on the painting spree with a friend during a vacation from law school. His father was away on business at the time.*

of the novelist, paid many a nighttime visit to Clarke, who had a wife and family in England. When her husband died in 1813 at the age of thirty-seven, Ann moved in with Clarke. A son was born eight months later, of one or the other father, and several more children followed. One of Cooper's most exciting Hyde Hall stories is probably a total fabrication. He said that when Ann's son George Clarke, Jr., married Anna Maria Gregory, the new mistress of Hyde Hall banished the old. He claimed that before Ann stepped into the carriage that bore her away, she called out to her son, "You may drive me out now, but I shall return and haunt [Hyde Hall] forever." And she added another curse for good measure: "May no woman ever be happy in it again." In fact, Ann had been dead for several years when George married Miss Gregory.

ABOVE AND RIGHT: *The elegant main staircase of Hyde Hall is a beautifully proportioned three-story spiral made of mahogany. Every sixth spindle is iron, giving the banister added support.*

Anna may not have been cursed, but she was unhappy. She never liked the country life and left George as a result. George, meanwhile, struggled with financial problems. Great Britain had freed its West Indian slaves in 1838, thus liberating Clarke's Jamaican labor force. His tenant farmers in New York were departing in droves for the rich lands of the Ohio Valley, leaving behind exhausted fields and rotting barns. Legal challenges to the validity of his inheritance dragged on for years. Fearing that he would lose all his inherited lands, he bought additional land with borrowed money, and borrowed again to speculate in the hops market. When the market crashed, George was ruined. With debts of one million dollars, he declared bankruptcy—the largest that had yet occurred in the country's history.

Hyde Hall was rescued by a group of friends who bought the house and four thousand acres at the bankruptcy sale, and by the woman who would be mistress of the house in one of its happiest times. George, Jr.'s son George Hyde Clarke, born in 1858, married Mary Gale Carter, a wealthy heiress, in 1885. At the bankruptcy auction she purchased all the furnishings with funds provided by her mother; a few years later she bought back the house itself and the land. One of the Clarkes' allies at the bankruptcy sale was young George's friend from Columbia law school, Toby Strong (the son of the famous diarist George Templeton Strong), who was invited to spend his summers at the mansion and virtually became a member of the family.

The Clarkes undertook some repairs to the house, which had suffered from neglect during the family's financial troubles, and proceeded happily into the Gilded Age. Although not as large or opulent as some of the new mansions of the Hudson Valley and Newport, Hyde Hall possessed a baronial atmosphere that other houses merely pretended to have. The pride and grandeur of the old days were restored, but an eeriness that seemed to have been built into the house was never quite expunged.

A wedding in 1907 inspired an enthusiastic passage in a book by Ralph Birdsall, rector of Cooperstown's Episcopal church: "Hyde Hall is at its best as the centre of a function, crowded with guests, buzzing with conversation, while the company overflows from the house to the lawn, presenting a kaleidoscope of color in the shifting throng." His description of the crowd may have been a disguised plea never to be left alone in this place. Writing of Hyde Hall's shadowy precincts, Birdsall borrowed the cadences of Poe: "rambling passages . . . halls that beckon amid dim lights to unrevealed recesses of space . . . deeper down into the spacious wine-cellars darkly festooned with cobwebs, and chill as the

ABOVE: *Another view of the bedroom that was originally the billiards room reveals its distinctive blue-green paint, dating from the 1920s.*

25

family burying-vault where vines and snakes squirm through bars of its iron grates beneath the hill."

George and Mary's oldest son occupied the house until 1962. The state of New York took the property by eminent domain to establish a park and planned to raze the mansion, but family members and preservationists saved it. Funds were slowly raised for a restoration project, which is under way. A few of the furnishings that were removed in the early 1960s have been returned to the formal rooms, restoring some of the home's early grandeur.

The rambling passages and dim, beckoning halls are indeed the eerie places Ralph Birdsall described. On paper the floor plan is straightforward, but something about this house quickly confuses the visitor. Moving from one of the large front rooms into the narrow halls and small rooms beyond is like stepping into a maze. The courtyard is even more disorienting. Intended as a means to bring light and air to the interior of the mansion, it has just one doorway, partly concealed behind a round turret. Once inside the courtyard, it is possible to feel that there is no way out. The walls are not quite parallel, making it seem as though they are closing in. The floor of the court is paved with stones that are now loose and askew, and sounds echo here with a dull heaviness. When the pavement was new, flat, and polished, sounds were probably sharpened in this enclosure. Crews working on the restoration found the shards of a Champagne glass in the courtyard drain, suggesting that on at least one occasion someone wanted to hear this box of stone echo with the bright, jolly sound of glass being smashed. An early-nineteenth-century beer bottle was found mortared into the side of the drain. Perhaps it was some workman's personal signature; perhaps George Clarke wished to have gaiety built into the very bones of Hyde Hall.

ABOVE: *The striking plasterwork of the drawing room features vines, garlands, and urns. The design of the frieze was based on illustrations in Asher Benjamin's* American Builder's Companion, *published in 1826. The sconces were made in the 1890s, probably by carpenters or tinsmiths who worked on the estate. The pier mirror is one of three George Clarke ordered for this room from a maker in New York.* OPPOSITE: *In George Clarke's dressing room and office, two paper cases with glass doors rest upon a handsome wardrobe, which was custom-made by a local cabinetmaker to fit into its alcove. The paper cases, made for Clarke's Albany town house, are being stored in the alcove temporarily. The statue, depicting Narcissus, is a bronze copy of a statue discovered at Pompeii in the 1850s. Mary Gale Carter Clarke brought it back from Naples as a souvenir in the 1880s.*

THE CHAPMAN HOTEL
NORTH BLENHEIM, NEW YORK

The Chapman Hotel has long been an object of curiosity in its remote stretch of Schoharie County. An attractive two-story yellow-and-green clapboard building, it sits by the side of a narrow, winding road that runs through rugged hills, along the Schoharie River, and through the tiny town of North Blenheim. The hotel preserves the atmosphere of the old days, with its worn and comfortable furniture, its small, unpretentious bar, its genial back-country hospitality, and its good food, cooked on a wood stove. It is the essence of coziness—the rooms are low-ceilinged, dimly lit, and fragrant with wood smoke. In the dimness the visitor is vaguely aware of being surrounded by a hodgepodge of remnants of other eras—stuffed bobcats and other hunting trophies, old jars, signs advertising defunct businesses, the high chair which the proprietor himself used seventy years ago. It does not seem that these things have been collected and arranged but that they have simply come to rest here. The hotel has been owned by the King family since 1928, when Orra and Blanche King bought it from Frank Chapman. It is now operated by Amos King, who was eleven when his family came here, and his wife, Mildred.

ABOVE: *The kitchen has two stoves, one a wood stove and the other a modern gas range, which Amos's mother could never bring herself to use.* RIGHT: *A Kalamazoo wood stove, in use here for about twenty years, is the source of the pies that have given Mildred her fame as a cook. The fragrance of its smoke fills the hotel. Mildred has already worn out two or three similar stoves.* OPPOSITE: *Some time in the early 1950s, when the Kings' children were born, they saved this calendar picture of a baby in cowboy gear. Since then the picture has been repeatedly varnished and shellacked along with the rest of the kitchen wall, becoming a permanent presence of childhood.*

Blanche did all the cooking until her death a few years ago, and now Mildred prepares the food.

The hotel's immediate charm and appeal naturally lead visitors to wonder how long the place has been in existence. Several people have looked into its origins, without success. The beginnings of the Chapman are well beyond the reach of any memories in Schoharie County—the hotel was here before the road was paved, before the covered bridge was built over the river, before there was electricity, perhaps before there was anything—and any documents that may exist to attach a date to the hotel's establishment have eluded local historians. The guest registers predating 1935 are long lost.

The earliest reference to the hotel is in an 1866 county atlas. Judging by its architectural style, which is vaguely

Greek Revival, the building itself was probably built in the 1820s or 1830s. A British traveler's account of a trip through the region in 1825 suggests that the hotel did not then exist. The traveler, named Finch, wrote of a beautiful but anxious sleigh ride through the valley, describing the "dark gloom" of the pine and fir forest on the "intensely cold" moonless night, with the woods faintly illuminated by snow and filled with the roaring echoes of a mountain stream which he could not see. "He dreaded to encounter the Hermits of Schoharie, men who, with an axe as their sole companion, penetrate into these forests to cut down the pine timber." The Schoharie hermits often descended upon travelers and relieved them of their possessions. Had the Chapman Hotel existed in 1825, Mr. Finch and his frightened driver would undoubtedly have taken refuge there for the night.

The Schoharie hills have long been home to tough characters. A county historian writing in 1882 said that the people of colonial times "presented a rougher edged morality than now, which perhaps produced more sensational pleasures, yet did little, if anything, to improve character [or] elevate society." During the anti-rent wars of the mid-1800s, when farmers openly fought landlords and lawmen, two sheriffs were kidnapped at a hotel near the Chapman by a gang disguised as Indians. It was the gang's intention to tar and feather the officers, but cooler heads prevailed. In this century these hills and forests provided cover for the clandestine operations of moonshiners and bootleggers. The gangster "Legs" Diamond ran a bootlegging business out of Catskill, some fifty miles away, and local farmers had their own stills in secluded spots around the Schoharie Valley. One of the regulars at the Chapman bar tells of recently discovering a hilltop cave concealing the rusted remains of a still.

Being a stop on the stage line between Middleburgh, Gilboa, and Grand Gorge—whence the railroad could take

ABOVE: *Located on a winding country road by the Schoharie River, the Chapman Hotel is owned by Amos and Mildred King. The Chapman's dining room has been serving home-cooked fare to travelers for well over a century.*

one to the wider world—the hotel was the valley's depot of news and gossip, a paradise for loungers on a winter's evening. Frank James, the son of the hotel's owner in the 1880s, described in his unpublished memoir "Folks and Places along the Schoharie" impromptu entertainments at the Chapman: "Gary Buckingham was famous for his stories and songs. . . . One of the Joslyn boys was a clever dancer and his 'hoe-downs' were 'knock-outs.' Others could do 'whistling' stunts and there were some real good fiddlers." The hotel had a pool table until a state official—"a wise guy," as Amos recalls—made them take it out for some obscure bureaucratic reason.

The ten guest rooms on the second floor that once accommodated stagecoach travelers are now used mainly

ABOVE, TOP: *Mildred's collection of Avon Christmas plates, which she began buying in 1972, hangs over the bay window in the dining room.* ABOVE, BOTTOM: *Beneath a stamped tin ceiling, the front sitting room displays the Kings' collections of bottles, jars, and clocks. Overnight guests register at the counter in front of the mirror. The hotel's small bar is reached through the doorway on the right.* LEFT: *An almanac from 1926 and an antique curling iron are pinned to a wall near the chalkboard listing the hotel's menu. An acquaintance fashioned a man out of springs, washers, a nut, and various scraps. The Kings do not know where the Egyptian lady came from nor do they know why she hangs upside down.*

during hunting season. At one end of the upstairs hall, a door swings open to reveal an enormous ballroom, once a premier gathering spot of the county, now a storage room. Amos's parents were proud that they kept illegal liquor out of the hotel during dances. "The town was full of bootleggers," says Amos. "They were so thick here in the street we quit running the dances. We were strictly 'no drink on the premises.'"

The Chapman has witnessed most of the important additions to the county. When electric lights were put in, the Kings accommodated the workers; when the road was paved, the new steel bridge built, and when dams were erected across the Schoharie, the workers stayed at the Chapman. The hotel has also seen some losses. The old part of the town of Gilboa no longer exists, having been inundated when the Schoharie Reservoir was built to provide additional capacity to New York City's water system, and in 1990 a propane gas explosion erased a good part of North Blenheim—"There was a town up there before they blew it up," says Amos.

Over the years numerous articles have appeared in newspapers and magazines about the Chapman. Writers are always asking Amos to reflect on the old days; but all the interviews have not turned him into a purveyor of ersatz profundities. He remains resolutely down-to-earth. "Being your place and always living here you don't think about it. Sixty years gone by here—hell, it's just a damned old hotel as far as I'm concerned. Some people love it, some people are scared." He then tells the story of the son who wanted to treat his mother to a short vacation at what they apparently thought was an elegant inn of the Bucks County or Berkshires sort. "They were strictly city, I guess. His mother wanted to stay here a week, and he wrote me a check. She went up that stairway and looked at them rooms, and I thought she was going to have a heart attack. I took him aside and said, 'Here's your money, you better find some different arrangements.'"

ABOVE: *Simple and clean, decorated with old wallpaper and furnished with antiques, the ten guest rooms of the Chapman Hotel are advertised as "smart and home-like."*

Amos has never considered upgrading his furnishings because he could never part with anything. Out-of-town guests are always asking if they can buy this or that piece, but Amos replies that he would feel lonesome if a particular favorite were taken away or that he just would not know how to fill the empty space. He has no idea how old anything is because it was all there in 1928 when his family moved in. He knows for certain that it is "furniture you won't find nowadays." In the front parlor is a homely calendar clock that is off by one day. Amos cannot see sending it out for repairs, but neither can he figure out how to readjust it. "When they get out of kilter, the calendar and the time, it's hard to get them back."

LEFT: *This oak bedroom set originally belonged to Amos's mother's family and came from California. It is now in one of the guest rooms.*

BANG HOUSE
SHARON SPRINGS, NEW YORK

he town of Sharon Springs extends along the sides of a ravine that cuts through the high ridge on the southern side of the Mohawk Valley. The road through town plunges and twists as it follows the bed of the ravine, passing the remnants of a nineteenth-century resort, a spa where New York, Boston, and Philadelphia society once came to take the waters. Amid thick woods on rugged hillsides are summer houses almost swallowed by overgrowth, boarded-up hotels, a stone church, carriage houses, and cottages, run-down but still standing.

As the road descends to the northern edge of town, the unmistakable odor of rotten eggs announces the presence of the sulphur springs. Over them stand the Imperial Baths, built in 1927 and recently closed, and alongside runs a magnesia spring that gushes up to form a creek. On the hilltop overlooking the creek is the house of Henry J. Bang, a New York City businessman who came to Sharon Springs in 1860 to make his fortune. Bang purchased the white frame house, originally a one-story building, from one of the town's founders; a subsequent owner enlarged it. A successful restaurateur and supplier of china and linens to hotels in the

city, Bang envisioned making a fortune by purchasing the magnesia spring and building an up-to-date health establishment that would attract guests from Europe.

It was believed that almost any disease could be at least temporarily relieved by a dose of the waters. The Indians had come to the springs for centuries, but it was not until 1825 that a white entrepreneur had the idea of opening a boardinghouse. In the next decade, a stagecoach line connected Sharon Springs with a railroad, signaling the real start of the resort. In 1857 the town doctor, Sebastian J. Fonda, published a book about the powers of the springs, noting their efficacy in treating such ailments as dyspepsia, asthma, nervous palpitations, neuralgia, rheumatism, diabetes, and catarrh. The waters of the sulphur spring—so sulphurous that it was said they could make one's clothing glow—were used chiefly for bathing. The waters of Bang's magnesia spring were imbibed to relieve internal ailments, and those of the third major spring were applied to the eyes.

Bang's complex of hotel and bathhouses, called Congress Hall, was an attractive establishment. In his *History of Schoharie County*, William Roscoe wrote that Bang "expended a large amount of money in beautifying the grounds; building arbors, temples, and laying out walks; building bathrooms and other improvements for the convenience and pleasure of visitors." The festive architectural centerpiece of the complex was an open-air "temple," its domed copper roof supported by sixteen spindly cast-iron columns and emblazoned with the name "MAGNESIA" in bold letters. In the shade of the temple, Bang's guests filled their glasses with the magnesia water that spouted from a fountain adorned with a pair of lions' heads. Either Bang or his architect was familiar with the classical world, because a similar pair of lions, in stone, guarded the Temple of Artemis, built in the second century B.C. in the Greek city of Magnesia.

The 1860s and 1870s were probably the zenith of the resort's fortunes. In those years Sharon Springs was a regular stopping place for the social elite—Vanderbilts, Van Rensselaers, and even Ward McAllister, the powerful arbiter of New York society. They and their companions in wealth came here in July before heading to Saratoga for the August racing season. They danced and dined, hunted and fished, went for carriage rides through the forest, and tended to their ailments; for the younger set, the springs provided a picturesque backdrop for romantic intrigues.

For Bang, however, his magnesia water was not quite the attraction that he hoped it would be—visitors preferred the more potent sulphur spring, owned by the rival Pavilion Hotel. By the mid-1870s, it was clear to Bang that his enter-

ABOVE, TOP: *Guests at Bang's hotel could pass the evening hours in this summer house, which originally had screens.*
ABOVE, BOTTOM: *The chains hanging from the ceiling of the summer house once supported swings.*

prise was failing. He removed the furniture from Congress Hall one day in 1875, and the next day the hotel caught fire. It is not definitely known that Bang himself struck the match, but if he did, his was only the first in what would be a long line of Sharon Springs insurance fires.

In the 1880s the resort began to lose its sparkle. The wealthy were then building their own elaborate summer houses in Newport, the Berkshires, and Saratoga, and were less interested in vacationing at a hotel. The owner of the Pavilion tried to keep his hotel attractive by offering the latest in spa technology from Europe, such as the "pulverization room," which was "an apartment where the visitor clothed in a rubber suit absorbs sulphur water forced into the room through pipes on the wall and atomized by steam or compressed air."

Despite this and other "famous and exhilarating methods," high society did not return. The resort was revived in the 1890s by a new clientele, well-to-do Germans, some of whom were involved in the brewing business. By the 1870s Sharon Springs had become a center for the region's growers of hops, and every fall representatives of the big brewing companies came up to inspect the hops harvest, an event that was celebrated with parties, athletic events, and dances called hops.

Bang sold his house to Max Schaefer, the "M" in F & M Schaefer Brewing Company. Finding the house a bit small for his needs, Schaefer had it jacked up, erected a new first floor beneath it, and surrounded the building with porches. The house remained in his family until 1987, and some of their wicker furniture remains in it today. Schaefer's great-grandsons, Frederick and Rudy Vom Saal, recall that Sharon Springs was a quiet place when they spent their summers here during World War I and the 1920s. One dramatic event of the 1920s which the Vom Saals remember was an

ABOVE, TOP: *The open-air Magnesia Temple was the center of Congress Hall's complex of hotel and bathhouses. Guests could fill their glasses here and then stroll through the beautifully manicured grounds.*
ABOVE, BOTTOM: *When Max Schaeffer acquired Bang's house in the 1870s he added a story and wraparound porches with a view of a wooded ravine. The Schaeffers were one of the well-to-do German families that brought new life to Sharon Springs in the last decades of the nineteenth century. Today, the house is being restored by a woman from California who hopes to bottle the waters of the magnesia spring on the property.*
OPPOSITE: *The waters of the magnesia spring once spurted from the mouths of these lions in Henry Bang's Magnesia Temple.*

invasion of rats, attributed by town officials to the laziness of hotel managers in sealing garbage containers. Their father was appointed Police Officer #1 (being the only one) to enforce the trash regulations. When one manager became belligerent with the new peace officer, Vom Saal (a collegiate swimming and gymnastics champion) knocked him flat, securing the immediate cooperation of all the hoteliers.

By the 1920s, increasing numbers of Jewish immigrants from Central and Eastern Europe were visiting the spa from their homes in New York City. Their patronage kept the bathhouses in business at a time when the popular belief in the effectiveness of water cures was waning in this country. These visitors, however, preferred to stay in inexpensive boardinghouses and cared little for the social and athletic events sponsored by the large hotels. In 1941 the venerable Pavilion Hotel was torn down. After World War II, Jewish refugees from Europe brought a new wave of business to Sharon Springs in large part because the treatments of Holocaust survivors were partly subsidized by the West German government.

Magnesia Temple, on private land, no longer provides the public with its refreshment, but across the road the Adler Hotel is refurbishing its baths, and a company has acquired a large piece of land with the intention of opening a bottling plant. It plans to begin wide distribution of the spa's water, which may result in a revival of the fame of what Dr. Fonda called the "sparkling and delicious beverage" of Sharon Springs.

ABOVE: *A toolshed on the edge of the property stands by the town's main road, which descends through a ravine and continues north into the Mohawk Valley.* OPPOSITE: *Gates and a patch of smooth ground are virtually all that is left of a tennis court built by Frederick Vom Saal in the 1920s. A champion athlete at Columbia Univer-sity, he entertained the children of Sharon Springs with his stunt of swimming great distances with only his toes showing above the water.*

GIBSON HOUSE
BOSTON, MASSACHUSETTS

In the winter of 1941, a photographer from *Life* magazine accompanied the author John P. Marquand as he toured landmarks of Brahmin Boston—the Athenaeum, Louisburg Square, Mount Vernon Street, the Common, and the second-floor library in the town house at 137 Beacon Street, the lair, refuge, and shrine of Charles Hammond Gibson, Jr. In the photograph Marquand sits at ease, arms and legs folded, while Gibson sits stiffly in his writing chair, head held at just the right angle to express courteous interest in a visitor's remarks. In his novels Marquand chronicled old Boston's decadence, and in this photograph he sits face to face with its embodiment. In a brief piece for *Life*, he wrote, "One of the old guard of Beacon Street was speaking sadly of the old days. He ended by remarking regretfully that there were no longer any quaint old characters in Boston. It never occurred to him that he was assuming that essential role and that time had marched on until he himself was a character." Quite possibly he was describing Gibson, because that is the kind of remark that Charlie was in the habit of making. But if Marquand was talking about Gibson, he was wrong in one important

respect—Charlie was acutely aware of his role as a living relic. It was a persona that he cultivated.

Charlie had already decided to make his house into a museum of the Victorian age. He wrote in 1938 that it was his plan to leave the house "as a literary shrine, the frame work, in an unusually complete condition, of the life work of a New England writer"—the writer being himself. He thought that his house represented "the higher standards of American letters, the arts, and the art of living, . . . intended to be a demonstration of the manner in which a typical family lived at that time, and their principles of character, good citizenship, and taste in living." Architecturally, the house is a typical example of mid-nineteenth-century town house design, and its furnishings are not exceptionally rich or rare. But Charlie's instincts were nonetheless correct. He predicted in the 1950s that by the end of the century Victorian survivors would be very few and very treasured.

Charlie preserved the High Victorian clutter of vases, ewers, knickknacks, and peacock feathers in urns; of pictures on tables, walls, and the tops of bookcases; of statuettes and piles of books. Carpets and curtains are richly patterned, and huge mirrors reflect the overstuffed, tasseled velvet chairs. Designed by Edward Clarke Cabot, the five-story attached house had been built by Charlie's widowed grandmother Catherine Hammond Gibson in 1860 and was one of the first residences built on the newly filled-in Back Bay. Mrs. Gibson probably decided to build there at the urging of her cousin Samuel Hammond Russell, who built the adjoining house, also designed by Cabot.

In 1871 Catherine's son Charles married Rosamond Warren, unifying two prominent Boston lineages, which included the Revolutionary patriot Joseph Warren (killed during the last British charge at Bunker Hill) as well as distinguished merchants, doctors, and philanthropists. After

ABOVE: *Oriental carpets are thrown over a plain blue Wilton carpet in the second-floor library, adding to the room's profusion of rich colors.* OPPOSITE: *This reclining Turkish tufted chair was the favorite of Charles, Jr., and his father. The younger Gibson referred to it as his Sleepy Hollow chair. Made in the 1870s or 1880s, it was of a type popularly known as the "opium chair" because it suited sleepy, drug-induced reveries. Many sorts of narcotics were used by all classes of society in the late nineteenth century; but there is no evidence that any of the Gibsons used them.*

OVERLEAF: *In 1890, Charles, Sr., oversaw the redecoration of the library, which also served as his home office and as the men's sitting room. He retained overstuffed Turkish furniture that was out of style and had a gold-toned burlap wallpaper put on the walls. The large portrait over the fireplace is a late addition to the house, depicting an unknown woman who is not a member of the Gibson family. The charcoal sketches of Charles, Jr., flanking the oil portrait were made when he was at St. Paul's School.*

their honeymoon the couple moved into Catherine's house, where Charles Hammond Gibson, Jr., was born in 1874. The senior Charles Gibson, who ran a cotton brokerage firm, was an avid sportsman and outdoorsman, fond of horses, hunting, sailing, bicycling, tennis, and golf. Rosamond was described by a relative as "always exquisite in her dress and manners, having an almost Louis Quinze appreciation of the value of correctness and the other social charms. . . . She was not only a brave spirit but was a great wit as well."

Young Charlie was placed on the educational rails that would take him toward a productive life—Saint Paul's School, MIT—but he gave up his architectural studies at MIT to travel to England in 1894 and assist in the preparation of the Jackson-Harmsworth polar expedition. With no need to earn his living, he headed to France for a tour of châteaux and gardens, which resulted in his first book, *Two Gentlemen in Touraine*. Written under the pseudonym of Richard Sudbury and published in 1899, it is the narrative of Charlie's travels through the province in the company of a French count. Full of his ruminations on art, politics, society, and the philosophy of life, *Two Gentlemen* reveals Charlie as a melancholy connoisseur of feelings, a geographer of the chasm between ideals and reality, a chasm that he would occupy for much of his life.

He wrote poetry for his entire adult life and regarded himself as the "chief exemplar of the ode in America" but received little attention from the critics and the public. He paid for the publication of his poetry books himself. He led an active social life and was a part of the intellectual circles surrounding Isabella Stewart Gardner and the collector and decorator Henry Davis Sleeper, whose house on the North Shore, Beauport, remains a showplace of art and antiques. Through Sleeper, Gibson may have met some of the notable

ABOVE: *With its red carpet and wallpaper and sturdy leather furniture, the third-floor study is among the most masculine rooms in the house. It had been the bedroom of Charles Gibson, Sr. (Mrs. Gibson slept in the adjacent room). The separate bedrooms of husband and wife were linked by a bell pull; either one could ring for the other. Charles, Jr., converted it into his study—a more private retreat than the second-floor library.* OPPOSITE: *The Turkish sofa came to the study during a redecoration of the house in 1890. It was part of a set that had been in the house from the start and had become unfashionable. Rosamond wanted to throw the set away but her husband, Charles, Sr., insisted on keeping it. He put an armchair from the set into his library and moved his cherished old sofa into his own bedroom. The drapery tossed on the sofa was originally in the music room.*

ABOVE: *A bronze pheasant in the dining room is a typical Victorian decoration. Paintings and sculptures of game were often displayed in dining rooms because it was thought that they enhanced the appetite. They also reflect the Victorian "genderization" of rooms—an allusion to hunting was appropriate in a dining room, which was regarded as masculine.* RIGHT: *The butler's pantry was linked to the kitchen pantry in the basement by a dumbwaiter; as a result, servants did not have to make their way up a narrow flight of stairs carrying trays of hot food. The pantry sink was made of copper, a relatively soft material, to minimize the breakage of porcelain during washing. Next to the sink is a portable tea set—pot, burner, tray, and cups—in a wicker basket, designed for picnics. Like other residents of the Back Bay, the Gibsons frequently went on picnics in the Public Garden or on the bank of the Charles.* OPPOSITE: *The great variety of china in the butler's pantry is typical of an upper middle class home of the period. Different patterns were called for depending on the degree of formality of the occasion. The family's finest china would not be stored here; it was displayed in the dining room.*

collectors of the day who visited Beauport, such as Henry Francis du Pont and John D. Rockefeller. At one time he stated that he was an interior decorator, but there is no indication that he received any commissions. He served for a time as an unpaid member on the Boston Park and Recreation Commission and stirred a minor controversy by building an octagonal granite comfort station, modeled on the Petit Trianon of Versailles, on Boston Common.

After his father's death in 1916, Charlie, then forty-two, moved back to 137 Beacon to be with his mother, with whom he enjoyed a very close relationship. He lived elsewhere for the decade between 1921 and 1931, then returned to 137 Beacon permanently. After his mother's death in 1934,

ABOVE, TOP: *On the library mantel, a tortoiseshell Louis XV clock, which Charles, Jr., acquired in France, is flanked by photographs of Charles and his mother taken at Forty Steps, the family's summer house in Nahant. They were photographed in the 1930s in Charles's rose garden, which was widely admired and heavily visited when Charles opened it to public view.* ABOVE, BOTTOM: *Inkstands, manuscripts, and other literary paraphernalia remain on Charles Gibson's desk in the library, lit by a pair of oil lamps converted to use electricity.*

he became the master of the house. He did not get along well with his two married sisters, who annoyed him by removing items from the house—or "ransacking" it, as Charlie put it—after their mother's death. He was already mulling over the idea of turning the house into a Victorian museum and wished everything to remain as it always had been.

By the 1930s proper Bostonians were abandoning the city, as the streetcar and automobile made it practical to reside year-round in one of the lush green suburbs and commute to the ancestral countinghouses on State Street. The town houses of the Back Bay were sold off and subdivided into apartments and boardinghouses. Charlie held on to his house, one of the dwindling number of single houses in the district, and became fanatical about preserving it. At tea and cocktail parties, no one was allowed to sit down because Charlie wanted the brocade upholstery to last forever. He made a detailed catalog of the furnishings in the library and music room, noting the locations of his manuscripts. (He intended to catalog the contents of the rest of the house, but never got around to it.) He also began to draw up a short inventory of his life—he wrote his own obituary. It is just the kind of document one of Marquand's Back Bay eccentrics would compose—comic, cranky, and condescending. He alluded to "intimate" friendships with the British royal family and to his prominence in New York, Newport, and Philadelphia society. He noted that the management of his inheritance took up some of his time but complained that he "detested [being] compelled to make money" on the stock exchanges.

Estranged from his sisters and their families, Charlie felt his emotional world shrinking in the 1930s and 1940s. As he sat alone on Christmas night, 1944, he wrote a poem called "The House of Gibson," in which melancholy mingles with a drop of self-deprecating humor.

For I am the head of the House of Gibson
And am a most fastidious person.
Not one in a million will do for me
To sit in the shade of the family tree.

With all of them gone, I am so alone
I am like an old dog that has lost its bone.
Like the last leaf on a family tree
Withered and worn, as you can see.

He said in the 1950s that the Back Bay had been "the essence of a refined and cultured society" and bemoaned the conversion of fine old homes into classroom buildings and boardinghouses. He opened Gibson House to the public,

ABOVE: *Atop a nesting table in the music room is a German lithophane lamp, whose shade is made up of pressed porcelain panels depicting Rococo genre scenes. It was probably acquired by a member of the family on a trip to Europe. The photograph on the table shows a Warren relative, dressed in Elizabethan garb for a tableau.* LEFT: *Rosamond redesigned the music room in 1890 in the fashionable mode, choosing to lighten the room. She had the original dark woodwork painted white. The table by the window, part of the dark Turkish set of furniture of which her husband was so fond, was also painted white. One of the clocks Charles, Jr., collected in France is displayed upon it. The Sheraton chairs were two of Rosamond's heirlooms; they had been in her family's house on Beacon Hill. Charles and Rosamond both played instruments and often put on musicales in this room for friends.*

charging a $2 admission, to show off the embossed and gilt wallpaper in the hall, his mother's thirteen-piece faux bamboo bedroom set, the framed letter from Princess Elizabeth (soon to be queen) thanking him for the poem of welcome he had written on the occasion of her visit in 1952, and an early-seventeenth-century painting of Cleopatra by the Bolognese painter Guido Reni. Facing capture by Roman legions, Cleopatra shut herself into her mausoleum with the intention of dying among her treasures—a course similar to the one Charlie took as his refined neighborhood was turned over to students and short-term renters. He died at home in 1954, just a few days short of his eightieth birthday. In his will he expressed his wish that the house become a museum. In the 1950s the Victorian style provoked only shudders. Boston would not appreciate his achievement in preserving the house, he told his lawyer, until the year 2000.

In one of the books he wrote as a young man, he obliquely predicted a disparaging judgment of himself, foresaw being dismissed as "light and aimless" by a society that judged people "only by their financial success or failure and could not see that they really lived another, higher life." Throughout his house, in various nooks and crannies, he left manuscripts and letters. He identified some of these repositories in his inventory, but other caches he either forgot to mention or deliberately kept secret. Perhaps he hoped a devoted twenty-first-century curator would care enough about Charles Hammond Gibson, Jr., to ferret out and piece together the scattered shards of an eccentric career.

OPPOSITE: *Indoor bathrooms were still unusual when the house was built in 1859. Back Bay residences had them because when the bay was filled to create the district, water and sewer lines were laid down. This bathroom, off Rosamond Gibson's bedroom, was remodeled around the turn of the century.*

SKOLFIELD-WHITTIER HOUSE
BRUNSWICK, MAINE

ABOVE: *The northern corner of the hall sitting room boasts such family heirlooms as this deer head, shot by Frank Whittier in the Maine woods, and a Chickering piano, a popular accoutrement of the upper middle class in the latter part of the eighteenth century. The stained glass along the stairway was added by the Skolfields during the home's 1880s renovation.* OPPOSITE: *This "glider," a sofa that swings on chains attached to its frame, used to sit on the summer sleeping porch. The porch had to be removed in the 1970s because it had deteriorated and was causing leaks; the couch now sits in one of the bedrooms.*

In 1925 Eugenie Whittier, a sixty-four-year-old widow, closed up her seventeen-room house in Brunswick and went to live with one of her daughters. Although Eugenie and her two daughters usually stayed at the house during the summers, they saw no reason to refurnish, redecorate, or remove anything. Aside from a few trivial changes, the house remained as it was when Eugenie turned the key in the lock in 1925. In the 1980s, when Eugenie's daughter Alice offered the house to the Pejepscot Historical Society, curators found a parlor that had not been changed since the 1880s, drawers stuffed with long-forgotten brands of mundane household items, ships' logs from the 1850s, Alice's kindergarten drawings, and a beaver hat Eugenie's father had bought in Liverpool in the 1870s, still in its original elegant leather case. When a photograph of the family taken in the hall in the 1890s was compared to the present-day room, every object was still there, down to the peacock feathers in the urn beneath the old portrait of Eugenie's grandfather, George Skolfield.

Eugenie's father, Alfred Skolfield, and uncle, Samuel Skolfield, built the house in the late 1850s and early 1860s.

They decided to build a double house, a single structure divided by a thick wall with separate quarters for two families. The brothers were both sea captains, away much of the time, and may have seen an advantage in having their families live next door to each other. (As it turned out, the next generation did not get along well, and one set of cousins went to court to bar the others from the backyard.) Alfred and Samuel built their home on a lot facing the town common, an appropriately prestigious address for two of the most solid citizens in this solid brick-and-mortar town. Their father, George, was a shipbuilder and the town's largest taxpayer, and the brothers had a thriving business carrying cotton from Southern ports to England.

Italianate in style, with a plain façade and a cupola,

ABOVE, TOP: *The Skolfield-Whittier House faces the town green of Brunswick. A double house with separate living quarters for two families, it was completed in the early 1860s by two Skolfield brothers.* ABOVE, BOTTOM: *As part of the redecoration of the parlor in the 1880s, the family installed chandeliers which they had purchased in Belgium.* LEFT: *Eugenie and her sister, Marie, painted the folding screen in the formal parlor with lilacs, pussy willow, and woodbine. They painted several other items of furniture in the house as well.* OPPOSITE: *The staircase was moved to create this reception room, an informal family sitting area, in the 1880s. In that era, in houses all over the country, relaxed "living halls" began to replace formal entrance halls that were designed to impress visitors. This room has remained unchanged since the 1890s.*

ABOVE, TOP: *A portrait of John Harward, a relative of Martha Skolfield, hangs in a corner of the dining room. A copper kettle is suspended on a frame shaped like the numeral "5." The word "O'clock" runs along the curve of the frame. This curious piece, made in England, reminds the household that five o'clock is tea time.* ABOVE, BOTTOM: *A Chinese folding screen in the dining room was probably acquired by Alfred Skolfield on one of his trips. The blue Chinese vase on the tripod is inexpensive export ware.*

the house was large for its site but not ostentatious. Nevertheless, something about it irked the town. When the house was under construction in 1858, a local newspaper commented, "Quite a difference of opinion prevails as to the style of architecture adopted, but if the owners are satisfied we see no reason why the public should not be." The construction work progressed so slowly that it became a town joke, and eventually, a nuisance. The paper reported that a man tripped on some loose wood in front of the house and grumbled that the town was wearing out a lot of shoe leather tramping over the rubble. For reasons unknown, an arsonist set fire to a shed behind the main house, doing no great damage. If citizens continued to bear ill feelings toward the house after it was completed, they must have been amused when the Skolfields had repeated problems with its location. In the 1860s, the town common was still being used as a cow pasture, and cows often wandered onto the Skolfield lawn, munching grass and stepping through flower beds, even taking their ease on the porch.

Unlike most ship captains, Alfred Skolfield took his wife and children along with him on his voyages. Eugenie was actually born on the water. Martha Skolfield gave birth to her in 1860 aboard the *John L. Dimmock* in Savannah harbor. The ship's hold had been filled, the papers were in order, and there was a schedule to keep; the *John L. Dimmock* could not be detained just because the captain's wife was in labor. Ill health forced Alfred to give up sailing in 1861. He moved his family into their half of the new house in 1862, but just four years later they moved to Liverpool, where they stayed for nineteen years. When the Skolfields returned in 1885, they redecorated the house, which had been rented out in their absence, purchasing new furniture and rugs from the Corey Company in Portland and arranging some English furnisings they had brought back with them. They

created more rooms by absorbing an adjacent carriage house and moved the main stairway to enlarge the downstairs hall into an informal sitting room. Alfred was helping to put on a new roof in 1891 when a scaffold collapsed, pitching him to the ground. He was partially paralyzed in the accident but lived another four years.

Eugenie, the Skolfields' oldest child, was the only one who married. In 1895 she wed Dr. Frank Whittier, who had to be one of the most energetic men in the state. Frank's brio had been instilled in him by a rigorous upbringing. He had been a sickly child, and his parents forced him to play beyond the point of exhaustion to improve his stamina. They apparently succeeded, for at Bowdoin College he played rugby, was a stalwart on the crew that set a collegiate record for the

ABOVE: *This leather sofa in the hall sitting room was one of the original furnishings purchased by the Skolfields when they built the house. It was removed from its place in the parlor when they redecorated the house in the 1880s. The leather has split badly, probably from temperature fluctuations in the house.* LEFT: *A medical bag sits next to the telephone in the downstairs hall of the Skolfield-Whittier House. Two of the Whittiers, Frank and his daughter Alice, were doctors. Alice was the first female pediatrician in Maine.*

OVERLEAF: *The cupola is the only place where the two halves of the double house are linked. Reached by stairways from each side of the house, it has a lofty view of Brunswick's main street and the town green. The leather box contains a beaver hat purchased in England.*

four-man shell, and was elected to Phi Beta Kappa. He wanted to go to law school, but the college offered him the job of manager of their new gymnasium. He accepted and in his spare time took courses in physical training at Harvard and attended the Maine Medical School, receiving his M.D. in 1889. In addition to specializing in physical training and hygiene, he did advanced work in bacteriology and pathology. He never slept more than a few hours a night. Frank and Eugenie's wedding ceremony took place at 7:15 in the morning and the rice was still in the air as they hustled to the station to catch their honeymoon train.

The couple moved into the Skolfield house. Their first child, Isabel, was born in 1896; Alice followed in 1898; and Charlotte, in 1903. Frank's many commitments kept him

ABOVE: *By the late 1970s, this faucet in the laundry room was the only one Dr. Alice Whittier was using during her summer visits to the house.* LEFT: *The kitchen wood stove was the culprit of a family tragedy— nine-year-old Charlotte Whittier was burned to death in 1912 when she tried to cook breakfast before anyone else had gotten out of bed.* OPPOSITE: *The Whittiers called this the daily dishes pantry. Their everyday china was an inexpensive ware in a pattern called Trafalgar. This sink was last used in 1924.*

ABOVE: *The pair of dolls with a face photographically imprinted on fabric were given to Isabel Whittier around the turn of the century.* RIGHT: *A bottle of drugstore cologne, dating to the 1940s or 1950s, was left on the edge of the tub, installed in the 1880s. The ceramic clock on the shelf was made in the late 1890s.* OPPOSITE: *The crib and wicker carriage in the nursery were used by the Whittiers in the 1890s and early 1900s.*

away from the house for most of the day and evening. A colleague remembered that the staff of Dr. Whittier's pathology lab was kept at work until the second Pullman train was heard arriving at the station at 2:00 a.m. Then Frank would be up early to carry out his duties as the town's milk inspector. By the late 1890s, he was one of the region's leading experts in bacteriology and microscopy, skills that made him useful in law enforcement. Through microscopic examination of a spent cartridge found at a crime scene, he was able to prove that it had been fired from the chief suspect's rifle. In another case he used a serum test to show that a blood sample was from a human and not an animal.

The entire family maintained a hectic pace of work and play. Alice wrote in her diary in 1911 that her activities, aside

from schoolwork, included weekly dancing lessons, twice-monthly meetings of the Misses Club, skating, bicycling, croquet, checkers, tennis, hide-and-seek, cooking, crocheting, and chair caning. Work was the therapy Alice chose to help ease the shock of a family tragedy. Early one January morning in 1912, nine-year-old Charlotte awoke before anyone else and tried to start breakfast on the wood stove in the kitchen. Screams roused the family, and Frank rushed to the kitchen to find his daughter's clothes in flames. His medical expertise could do nothing to save her and she died of her burns in a few hours. Alice described the incident to a historian seventy years later, remembering that she was determined to go right back to school rather than spend any time in mourning, a decision she regretted for the rest of her life.

ABOVE: *A stereopticon in the parlor is set up with a photograph of Carrick-a-Rede Gorge in Ireland, published in 1903. The conch shell may have been acquired by Alfred Skolfield on one of his voyages. An inscription on it says that it was engraved with a pen knife, and that the portrait is of "Omar Pacha Commander in Chief of the Ottoman Empire." It also has a rendering of the SS* Himalaya. LEFT AND OPPOSITE: *One of the bedrooms has a fine set of Eastlake furniture. When the Skolfields redecorated the house in the 1880s they purchased a number of pieces in the Eastlake style.* LEFT: *Eugenie and her sister painted the flowers on the back of the washstand.* OPPOSITE: *Fresh hydrangeas grace an Eastlake side table. The lace curtains were purchased in Liverpool, where the family resided for many years.*

ABOVE, TOP: *The desk in the library contains the records of Alfred Skolfield's seafaring career, such as business documents, ships' logs, and cargo manifests. The blackface figure on the desk is a mechanical bank that tosses coins from hand to mouth. The large portrait on the wall is of Frank's father, Nathaniel Whittier.* ABOVE, BOTTOM: *The Eastlake bed in the front bedroom has a bed covering that is one of the newer items in the house; it was purchased by Isabel Whittier in the mid-1900s. By the windows is the glider that was formerly on the sleeping porch.* OPPOSITE: *When the Skolfields returned to Brunswick after a long residence in England, they installed an English-style bathroom, with three separate chambers for a bathtub, toilet and sink, and slop hopper, into which chamber pots were emptied in the morning.*

The two surviving Whittier sisters both attended Bryn Mawr, and both chose careers working with young people, Isabel as a teacher and Alice as a pediatrician. Alice enrolled at Yale Medical School. She was coming home from Yale for Christmas in 1924 when the stationmaster in Brunswick told her that her father had suffered a heart attack on the train to Portland and had died on the spot.

It was in the following spring that Eugenie decided to close up the house and live with her daughters. It was not a settled life at first, because Isabel and Alice moved around quite a lot, pursuing their careers. Isabel taught in a high school in Pennsylvania, a junior college in Washington, D.C., at Hunter College in New York City, and in 1930 joined the faculty of Brooklyn College, where she taught European history until 1962. She traveled frequently and wrote children's books. After receiving her medical degree from Yale in 1925, Alice worked in Worcester, New Haven, Philadelphia, Chicago, and New York City. In 1930 she set up a practice in Portland as Maine's first female pediatrician.

The Whittiers made only a handful of changes during their summer visits to the Brunswick house—Alice put a refrigerator in the laundry room and a few essential repairs were made. Left untouched was a large crack in the breakfast room wall, made many decades before when the girls climbed up the mantel and it fell over. Their father had never gotten around to fixing the crack, and it had become part of the fabric of the house. Throughout the house the sisters put knickknacks and souvenirs of their travels. Isabel, a good friend of Senator Margaret Chase Smith, collected all manner of Smith campaign memorabilia and left it in drawers, on mantels and dressers, and in closets.

A tiny room on the second floor is filled with their father's books, magazines, records, and medical instruments. On the floor lies an Indian club, of the sort once used in

gymnasiums, with a mystery attached. It is thought that the club may have been a murder weapon and that a dark stain on it is blood, which Frank was called upon to examine. A closet is jammed with small glass trays containing specimens that, if anyone ever cared to study them, would probably tell the medical tales of half the state.

Before Eugenie died in 1951, Alice interviewed her to get a description of each piece of furniture—who bought it, where, and when. Already aware that the house was an important historical artifact, Alice neatly bundled up more than a century's worth of odds and ends that had accumulated in the attic. There are packages marked "pink and white leggings 1908," "quilts," "colored feathers," and a bundle poignantly marked "Charlotte's socks," along with *Life* magazines, newspapers with headlines about the Korean War, and dozens of leather trunks bearing the labels of long-defunct railroads and steamship lines.

A portrait of George Skolfield, who helped build the house but never lived in it, has a prominent place in the hall. One winter's night a ghostly presence of some sort was either trying to pay him homage or simply trying to get a close look at the old shipmaster. The alarm sounded, and when the police and the curator arrived, they found a door mysteriously unlocked and the light on over George's portrait. The curator turned off the light and locked the door, only to return the next morning and find the light on again. As the light also illuminates the stairway, it is possible that the shade was making its way upstairs to the pile of specimens in the doctor's study, there to retrieve the particle of evidence that will prove someone's guilt or, one likes to think, innocence, in the court from which there is no appeal.

ABOVE: *One of the toys in the nursery of the Skolfield-Whittier House is a mechanical sailor who scrambles up a mast whenever he is pulled down to the bottom—just the sort of toy one would expect seafaring parents to buy for their children.* OPPOSITE: *Dr. Alice Whittier neatly bundled and labeled many of the family's possessions in the attic.*

THE
SOUTH

AIKEN-RHETT HOUSE
CHARLESTON, SOUTH CAROLINA

In his chronicle of the upper class, *The Saga of American Society*, Dixon Wecter wrote that "Charleston has a gay, quixotic contempt for great riches." He was writing in the 1930s, when many of the old families of Charleston were selling ancestral lands and houses they could no longer afford to maintain. The Rhett family, however, had been fortunate enough to hold on to the wealth their forebears had acquired in the prosperous era before the Civil War, and their mansion on Elizabeth Street, the Aiken-Rhett House, remained in the family until the mid-1970s.

Some of South Carolina's grandest entertainments were held in the house before and during the Civil War, but in this century the Rhetts lived quietly and unostentatiously. From 1918 until 1932, the occupants of the fourteen-room mansion were two bachelor brothers, I'on and Burnet Rhett, who refused to modernize it (they did concede to electricity in a couple of rooms and to an indoor bathroom but not to a new kitchen or central heating) and used fewer and fewer of the rooms as their needs shrank. Waited upon by a large household staff, they spent their days mostly in the dining room, having their meals, enjoying their pipes, brandy, and conver-

ABOVE: *The original entrance to the house was on this side. The house was constructed as a double house between 1817 and 1820, and redesigned by William and Harriet Aiken in the 1830s as a single house. They had acquired the house as payment of a debt.* OPPOSITE: *A curving double stairway of marble ascends from the Elizabeth Street doorway. The cast-iron balustrade is decorated with an acanthus motif. This sumptuous Greek Revival entrance hall was added in the 1830s.*

sation, and growing old, stodgy, and contented. I'on (which rhymes with lion) carried on a long courtship with Frances Dill. After about twenty-five years of courting, they were married in 1932. I'on was fifty-five. It was not until 1952 that Frances had a new kitchen put in, at last ending the old practice of cooking in the outdoor kitchen behind the house. After I'on died in 1959, Frances stayed on with a couple of servants, using even fewer rooms. In 1972 her sister persuaded her to move out. The house stood empty, preyed upon by vandals, until The Charleston Museum agreed to acquire it in 1976.

When the house was opened to visitors, Charleston discovered what a great treasure had been sitting unrecognized in its midst. The house was filled with furniture and art objects of an era long gone. Wallpaper put up in the 1830s was clinging precariously to the walls, but it was still there, as were the beds, tables, chairs, portraits, and artwork that had been used by generations of the Aiken and Rhett families.

The house stands in what was once the suburb of Wraggsborough, now part of the city of Charleston. It was built by a wealthy cotton factor named John Robinson between 1817 and 1820 as a double house in the Federal style. Robinson lost his property in the 1820s to creditors, one of whom was William Aiken, Sr. He had come to Charleston from Ireland as a child in 1789, later prospered in the cotton business, and helped to start the South Carolina Canal and Railroad Company. After his death in a carriage accident in 1831, his only child, William, Jr., took possession of the house and the Aiken businesses. He and his wife, Harriet, redesigned the house between 1833 and 1836, making it into a showplace of the Greek Revival style. They shifted the entrance from Judith Street to Elizabeth Street and built a grand entrance hall, with a cantilevered marble stairway decorated with cast-iron rails; removed a hallway in order to create a double parlor with mahogany pocket doors; and installed

marble mantels they had purchased in Italy and gilt chandeliers from Paris. Other items were ordered from New York.
When it was finished the house became the headquarters for
William Aiken's campaign for the state legislature. He won a
seat in 1838, was elected governor by the legislature in 1844,
and represented South Carolina in the U.S. Congress from
1851 to 1856. By this time he was the largest slaveholder in
the state and one of its wealthiest citizens.

After another tour of Europe in 1857, the Aikens
redecorated the house in the Rococo Revival style, adding an
art gallery to display paintings and sculptures. In Florence
they purchased some copies, made by American art students, of famous statues such as Canova's Venus and a
reclining Mary Magdalene. They also bought a classical-style

ABOVE: *This early-nineteenth-century
writing table in a second-floor bedroom is a
transitional piece between the Hepplewhite
and Empire styles. The mirror is decorated
with sunbursts.* LEFT: *A large English
Regency bookcase dominates the upstairs
hall, where portraits of Daniel Webster,
Henry Clay, and John C. Calhoun have been
hung.* OPPOSITE: *The tall case clock has a
mechanism made in Charleston in 1835; the
case itself is probably English. The ball at its
foot is a counterweight from one of the
house's whale-oil lamps, which were lowered
by means of a pulley to replenish their fuel.
The room beyond is the library, with a sten-
ciled sofa from 1825.*

OVERLEAF: *Henrietta and Major Burnet
Rhett slept in this sleigh bed, probably made
in New York in the 1840s.*

ABOVE: A sentimental statue of a shepherd boy stands in the corner of the salon. Sculpted by E. S. Bartholemew, an American artist living in Florence, it was purchased by the Rhetts during a trip to Italy in 1857. The silk damask couch dates to 1840 and the English harp-lute to about 1810. RIGHT: A pair of gilded mirrors, made in New York in the 1830s, pass their reflections back and forth to infinity in Harriet Aiken's bedroom. Shreds of the original wallpaper still cling to the walls. The date of the French clock on the mantel is not known. The oil-burning lamps with crystal pendants were made in the mid-1800s. OPPOSITE: A bust by Hiram Powers occupies a corner of the salon next to a cast-iron and ormolu candle stand. One of a set of four, the stand was purchased in Paris.

bust by the American artist Hiram Powers, whose statue of a naked and chained Greek slave had created a scandal when it was displayed in Washington, D.C.

Perhaps the most powerful work of art in the house is the huge portrait of Harriet Aiken in the salon, surrounded by a gilded frame and flanked by large gilded mirrors. It was done in 1856 by the local artist George Flagg. Exquisitely beautiful and elegantly dressed, Mrs. Aiken casts a determined gaze across her salon, toward a crystal and gilt chandelier she purchased in Paris, at whose top, on a crystalline setting, floats a golden crown. Both Harriet and her daughter, Henrietta, displayed the loftiness that comes with a substantial net worth. On a visit to Paris in 1848, when the city was torn by riots as a new republic was being formed,

Harriet complained that the street fighting was disrupting her social schedule. When Henrietta was being married to Major Andrew Burnet Rhett at the family's house in North Carolina in 1863, the bridal chamber caught fire during the ceremony. Completely undeterred, the Aiken women had the service continued as their servants dealt with the flames. The incident at the wedding was described by Mary Chesnut in her diary of the Civil War years. She commented sharply on the decorations at the country house, noting that Henrietta's dressing table was not draped with a simple fabric reflecting "honest, war-driven poverty" but with muslin and lace that were "a millionaire's attempt at appearing economical." It was this millionaire's muslin that caught fire.

The Aikens entertained Confederate president Jefferson Davis for a week in 1863 at their Charleston mansion, where Davis was delighted by his hosts' "perfect old Carolina style of living," in Chesnut's phrase. According to Chesnut, Davis was especially taken by "those old grey-haired darkies and their noiseless, automatic service, the result of finished training—one does miss that sort of thing when away from home." General Pierre G. T. Beauregard used the house as his headquarters for nearly five months when the Federal bombardment of the city drove him from his offices by the harbor.

Aiken was not the governor during the war and had opposed secession, but he was arrested after the war and confined for a short time in Washington. His fortune survived the war because he had made investments in Europe. Fearing that his money would be confiscated, he did not reclaim it right away. To provide necessities for the household, Harriet sold some of her jewelry. One of these necessities was a new piano for Henrietta. After the war Harriet obviously no longer cared about maintaining an economical appearance.

William Aiken lived until 1887, long enough to see his tranquil prewar term as governor recalled fondly as a golden

ABOVE, TOP: *This small table in Mrs. Aiken's room is part of her set of New Orleans furniture. Nothing is known about the painting, which probably dates to the mid-1800s.* ABOVE, BOTTOM: *Harriet Aiken's bedroom, closed off after her death in 1892, was left untouched until the 1970s, when the Charleston Museum acquired the house. When a curator entered for the first time, the air in the room was filled with a choking black dust. The room has since been cleaned. Its set of rosewood furniture is in the style of the New Orleans maker Prudent Mallard.* OPPOSITE: *The elaborate bed and mirrored wardrobe in Harriet Aiken's room are part of the set that may have been made by Mallard.*

ABOVE: *In the library, which has lost large sections of its plaster, there is a bust of Mrs. Joseph Daniel Aiken, fashioned after a plaster bust done by her husband, and a portrait of William Aiken, Jr., done in 1886, when he was eighty. The artist is not known. The bronze whale-oil lamp bears the inscription "Paris 1833."* OPPOSITE: *One of the bedrooms has a pre–Civil War bed whose posts are decorated with acanthus-leaf carvings. During the war General Beauregard used the house as his headquarters, but it is not known if he ever slept there.*

age. When Harriet died five years later, Henrietta closed off her mother's room and apparently vowed never to alter anything in the house that her mother had touched. When Henrietta Rhett died in 1918 her children paid her the same compliment. Her daughters were married, and the house passed to her two bachelor sons, I'on and Burnet. They remained in the house despite the fact that the Wraggsborough district, once a smart suburb, had deteriorated until it could only be described as a slum. Economic depression hit Charleston and the rest of the South when the boll weevil infestation of the early 1920s devastated the cotton fields. As some of the city's great mansions were being demolished to build parking lots and gas stations, northern museums and private collectors descended on Charleston to buy paintings, statues, and paneling from families desperate to raise cash. The Rhetts were able to avoid the depredations of the Yankee connoisseurs because they still retained the fortune that Governor Aiken had built up before the war, but they never spent any substantial sums on the house. A casual visitor would think that they were as poor as the rest of the city. When I'on Rhett died in 1959, Frances declined at first to move in with relatives, preferring to carry on amid the antebellum ormolu, tortoiseshell, and brass. She simply closed the rooms she did not need.

In 1975 J. Kenneth Jones, a curator from the Charleston Museum, made the first official museum visit to the house in the company of two family members who carried a "formidable" box of keys in "every size, every shape, every material," as Jones later wrote. With broken glass crunching underfoot, they picked their way through "the dark maze" of the first floor. Through closed shutters the tendrils of vines reached in from outside. Broken chains of prisms hung from chandeliers. Rotting silk drapery clung to gilded poles. Silver hardware had turned black, and a heavy black dust covered

ABOVE: One of the remarkable aspects of the Aiken-Rhett House is that it preserved many of its original outbuildings, including the slave quarters in the rear of the house. RIGHT: Furniture which curators have removed from downstairs rooms is stored on the third floor. When General Beauregard used the house as his headquarters he could have viewed activity in Charleston harbor from these windows. OPPOSITE: The slave quarters, built after a slave uprising of the 1820s, were designed with security in mind. The rooms are located off a long and narrow corridor. An overseer standing at one end of the hall with a gun could keep all the occupants at bay. It was certainly not a pleasant dwelling.

everything and hung in the air, so thick in one room that they could not breathe. In a storeroom they found old sheet music, a litter of books and papers, and a bundle wrapped in newspaper that contained an annotated copy of the original draft of the Confederate constitution, with notes taken during the constitutional convention by Robert Barnwell Rhett. The house was a rare, astonishing window on the past, but it was rarer still as a picture of the methods and maneuvers of decay, a tableau of the passage of time, where the years had been left alone to do their work, to make the neat arc in a cracked mirror, the whimsical fault lines in tired plaster, the lazy curls of paper getting free of the wall, a rich dust of Parisian gilt.

COOLMORE
TARBORO, NORTH CAROLINA

In talking with the Powells of Coolmore about their family, it is difficult, at first, to keep track of the generations and centuries—it seems that somehow a generation is being left out. Three Powells live at Coolmore today, Joseph C. Powell, his sister Mary, and Joseph's wife, Elizabeth. The siblings are in their eighties. When they speak of the Civil War, they refer to their uncles being killed and to their father being left as the only child in the family. Time has moved very slowly at Coolmore, and only one generation has passed in this house since the Civil War.

Coolmore stands on what was once the main road between the small town of Tarboro and Rocky Mount, one of the important milling and shipping centers of eastern North Carolina. For the better part of two centuries, the area has produced rich crops of cotton, tobacco, soybeans, grains, and dairy products. The house was built in the late 1850s by the Powells' grandfather, Dr. Joseph J. W. Powell, who inherited the Coolmore lands from his uncle, Richard Harrison, one of the richest men in Edgecombe County. A series of deaths in Harrison's family had left him with no heirs. "He lost his wife and his two little girls," Joseph explains. "He had a grown son

who was run over by a mule and killed. That left him by himself, so he asked my grandfather to come over from Halifax County and live with him, and said that he would leave him this property when he died. So he came over here with his family about 1852. I think Uncle Dick died about 1856, and so my grandfather started this house in '57."

With a substantial income at his disposal (the family records show an $80,000 purchase of slaves), Dr. Powell hired a Baltimore architect, Edmund G. Lind, to build the villa-style residence, with ten major rooms handsomely decorated and furnished, for a fee of about $20,000. A local newspaper reported that "for elegance and convenience [Coolmore] must have excelled any country residence in the State."

The two front parlors—one for the ladies and the other

ABOVE: *The mirror frame in the ladies' parlor still shows the damage that resulted when it was hastily removed from the house before the arrival of a Union raiding party. Mirrors and the family silver were taken to a hiding place some fifty miles away.* LEFT: *Coolmore's grand entrance harkens back to days of opulence. Facing one another are the gentlemen's parlor to the left and the ladies' parlor to the right. The cane and hat rack has been in the house as long as its owner can remember. The hanging flower lamp replaced the hall's original gas light.* OPPOSITE: *The ceiling of the entrance hall features superb plaster brackets and a medallion.*

ABOVE: *Delicate frescoes still grace the curved walls of the grand entrance hall. An exquisite faux-marble niche, for which a statue was intended originally, now holds a vase made by Mary Powell's sister. Below the niche is a cuspidor; several are still placed in the gentlemen's parlor and around the house. The elaborate floor is actually a hand-painted floor cloth. The doorway provides a glimpse of the ladies' parlor.* RIGHT: *The Gothic trefoils and quatrefoils in a chair back stand out against the frescoes of the entrance hall.* OPPOSITE: *The gentlemen's parlor, off the entrance hall, retains all its original furnishing from the early 1860s. The rich, bold pattern of the carpet was not considered showy at that time. In a letter in the family's collection, the dealer who acquired the carpets for the house states that he avoided "those flashy patterns."*

for the gentlemen—have never been changed except for the replacement of the curtains. The ladies' parlor still has its rosewood and French satin damask furniture; the gentlemen's parlor, its black walnut furniture. Both rooms have ceilings inlaid with gold decorations and large mirrors. The frame of the mirror in the ladies' parlor was broken when it was removed and hidden during the war. "They took the mirrors down," Mary Powell says. "I guess they considered them one of the important items . . . and sent them to a relative's house in Nash County, where they had sent the silver and other valuables." In the gentlemen's parlor is a bronze statue of Richard I on the mantel, an edition of Tennyson with an elaborate plated cover on a table, and a fine rosewood pianoforte. "The piano was given to my grandmother on her seventeenth

birthday, so it's actually older than the house." Music was one of the few avocations available to a nineteenth-century woman, whose chief role was running the home. "They didn't do very much for women in those days," Mary says.

In decorating the formal parlors with dark woods, gilding, and Rococo Revival flourishes here and there, Dr. Powell's architect remained entirely within the bounds of mid-Victorian taste. However, his decoration of the stair hall —a dim cylindrical room in which an elliptical staircase spirals up three stories to a cupola fitted with panes of colored glass—is an exquisitely pleasant hallucination, a dream of color, shapes, and muted light. On the first floor, the walls and underside of the staircase look paneled, but the moldings follow the curves of the walls and stairs with impossibly

ABOVE: *The rosewood piano in the gentlemen's parlor is older than the house. It was given to Martha Whitaker Powell on her seventeenth birthday in 1837. A framed box of handmade wax flowers is displayed atop the piano.* LEFT: *A set of steel engravings of biblical scenes by Raphael, printed in England, hangs in the gentlemen's parlor. The dealer who bought the engravings for Dr. Powell assured him that only one thousand sets would be sent to the United States—"This mitigates against their being common."* OPPOSITE: *The original wool and silk drapery of the gentlemen's parlor has survived remarkably well, while the red silk damask of the sofa has become so worn that the black background shows through.*

RIGHT: *The trompe l'oeil frescoes of the stair hall are a triumph of painting. Among all the papers at Coolmore relating to the construction of the house, there is no mention of the artists who created the stair hall. The staircase, fashioned of black walnut, took three months to construct. Many family weddings have taken place here because, according to Mary Powell, "everybody in the family wants to come down those stairs."*
OPPOSITE: *A wrought-iron statue of Mercury holds a lamp on the newel post of the staircase. The niches were meant to hold other statues, whose delivery from Europe was prevented by the outbreak of the Civil War.*

perfect fluidity. In fact, the walls are not covered in wooden paneling but are painted with trompe l'oeil frescoes, a delicate illusion in pale blue and beige. In Coolmore's adagio movement of time, the frescoes have remained marvelously fresh.

Almost as soon as the house was finished, Dr. Powell died. As Joseph recalls, "My grandfather lived here just six months and died. That left my grandmother and the two older boys, who were caught in the war. They went together. One was in prep school and one was in military school, VMI." Martha Powell gave birth to her third son, Joseph, in 1861. Her second son, Henry, was seventeen when he signed up for the cavalry in February 1864; the oldest, Richard, was nineteen. Their photographs hang in the ladies' parlor, where a scrapbook is kept with a letter from Henry to his mother:

August 18, 1864
camp below chafins bluff

Dear Mother,
    I wrote to you day before yesterday and just as I finished the bugle blew to saddling up and we went back where we had the fight the day before and had the hardest fight on tuesday that I ever was in. we didn't loose maney men, none in our company. we drove the yankees about 3 miles, took about 100 prissoners and 25 horses. general chambliss was killed.

On the same page of the scrapbook is a notice cut from the Rocky Mount newspaper:

Was killed on the 21st day of August while acting as one of the advance vedettes to his regiment, 3rd North Carolina Cavalry, near Poplar Spring Church in Virginia, Henry W. Powell. Death selects the shining mark at which to fling his insatiable arrow. Born November 12, 1846, was killed the 21st of August, so he fell under 18 years of age.

His brother Richard died at the very end of the war, as Joseph relates: "He was killed the last day. The war stopped one day, and he was killed the next day, before they got the word to all the troops that the war was over. . . . And so that just left my father, who was then four years old. No slaves and no help. And the economy was gone."

In the final days of the war, a detachment from Sherman's army landed at New Bern with orders to destroy the big cotton mills at Rocky Mount as well as any cotton gins they could find along the way; but, as along the route of Sherman's army in Georgia, South Carolina, and the rest of North Carolina, the officers and men were more or less free to destroy whatever they wished. As a child Mary Powell heard the story of what happened when a group of soldiers turned up at Coolmore. "Everybody had left but the house-

ABOVE: *The silk and wool drapery in the parlors used to be backed by curtains of Nottingham lace, which deteriorated and had to be removed. In summer the heavy drapes would be taken down, leaving only the lace to cover the windows.*

keeper. The story is that they considered burning it because it was too fine a house for 'an old Southerner' to live in. And some soldier stepped up and said, 'Oh please don't burn it because I worked on this house, and I expect to come back here and *live* in it.' So they didn't burn it." A former slave, Louise Battle, told a slight variation of the story to a newspaper reporter in 1937 when, according to the newspaper, she was almost one hundred years old. She said the Yankee wanted to save the house because he had never been paid for his work on the place. (She added that for three days the Yankees were "thick as flies in a molasses pot.") Mary Powell tends to discount the story, but her brother believes it. The architect may well have sent some craftsmen from Baltimore to carry out some of what Joseph calls "the fancy work."

ABOVE: *The rear entrance room, furnished with comfortable chairs, once had a painted-cloth floor covering, which wore out completely. The door gives access to a screened porch where the family entertains visitors in summer.* LEFT: *A closet in the dining room holds the family's French china, which does not bear a maker's mark. The Powells' collection of silver plate is also not marked.*

In the aftermath of the war, Dr. Powell's widow, Martha, was able to hold on to most of her land. She shifted away from a dependence on cotton and began dairy farming, as did a number of other people in the area. Against the odds, she prospered. In the 1880s her surviving son, J. C. Powell, the father of the current occupants, took over the management of the farm. He took a trip to Great Britain where, the family believes, he heard of an Irish farm named Coolmore and decided to adopt that name for his own farm, which had theretofore been called simply "Home Place."

In the early 1890s, the farm was flourishing. A writer for the Tarboro newspaper paid a call at Coolmore and wrote an article recalling what the county had lost because of the war and noting the gradual improvement that was taking hold in the region. He praised J. C. Powell's "fat cattle and thrifty hogs, his splendid mules" and remarked upon the "absolute cleanliness" of the dairy operation and the resulting purity of Coolmore's butter: "This butter can be eaten with your eyes shut, with no fear of eating anything but butter itself."

J. C. married when he was in his forties, and died a few years later in 1906. When his son Joseph grew up, he took over the farm, planting cotton, tobacco, corn, and small grains and raising cattle. He also worked as the county extension agent, receiving wide praise for his skillful advice. Mary had a long career in education. During World War II, she served in the Red Cross, managing recreational facilities "to keep the soldiers out of the bars." Except during the war years, she spent her summers at Coolmore and retired to the house in 1969.

When asked why they never made any substantial changes to Coolmore, Mary and Joseph look startled. Joseph replies, "We never had any occasion to change it." Mary laughs and says, "I think the pattern had already been set."

ABOVE: *A country villa in the Italianate style, Coolmore was completed in 1860 and has been occupied by the builder's family ever since. The house barely survived destruction by a Federal raiding party during the Civil War.* OPPOSITE: *Elaborately carved woodwork adorns Coolmore's front door. It opens onto a porch which originally was uncovered and extended further around the house. Owing to the shortage of help after the Civil War, it was shortened and roofed for easier maintenance.*

WOODLANDS
NORTHEASTERN GEORGIA

ABOVE: *A heavy iron bench, cast in the shape of leaves and branches, rests in the hallway of Woodlands, a summer house built by George Jones Kollock.* OPPOSITE: *A sunny bay window looks out from a downstairs bedroom to the garden. The slats of the window seat form a sunburst pattern.*

$\mathcal{A}$t the top of a heavily wooded hill in northeastern Georgia, the trees part to reveal a misty panorama of Georgia's Blue Ridge, with hump-backed Yonah Mountain dominating the view. In this hilltop clearing, George Jones Kollock, a cotton planter, built a Gothic Revival summer house for his family in the late 1840s. Called Woodlands, its sharp, weather-beaten gable ascends from a dense mass of ancient wisteria, protruding straight out from the front of the house like the brim of a cap, shrouding the porch in cool, green shade.

Kollock descendants still use the house, but to a visitor walking through the rooms alone it seems that the house's true occupants are a set of Confederate portraits that have been here since the Civil War. In the dining room is *The Last Meeting,* a sentimental print showing Stonewall Jackson and Robert E. Lee before the battle of Chancellorsville, in which Jackson was mortally wounded. A broadside of Robert E. Lee's farewell address to the Army of Northern Virginia, given at Appomattox, hangs on the wall of a downstairs bedroom. In the library a large engraving of Jefferson Davis scowls from atop a battlemented Gothic Revival book-

ABOVE, TOP: *The "grandmother's rocker" on the porch has been at Woodlands at least since the 1920s. Catharine's grandmother used it and now Catharine herself has inherited the honor of sitting in it—any other occupant must yield the chair when grandmother appears on the porch.* ABOVE, BOTTOM: *The slave quarters behind Woodlands were built at the same time as the main house in the same Gothic Revival style. The architecturally jarring Greek Revival columns, added later, are mementoes of a lost house. They were saved from Sleepy Hollow, the house built by George Kollock's brother, when that place was being torn down.* RIGHT: *A tiny child's chair and chamber pot stand beside a youth bed in an upstairs bedroom known as the "big front room." A crib is just visible next to the doorway.*

case. The shelves are filled with books, shells, Indian artifacts, rocks, and stuffed birds collected over a century ago.

More than just a place of shady cool, the mountains of northeastern Georgia were a refuge from the plagues of yellow fever that periodically struck the low-lying coast. It is almost impossible now to understand fully the euphoria that people felt when they arrived in the highlands, because there is little in the modern experience to match the terror that drove them there. "You are aware that yellow fever has made its appearance in Savannah," wrote George Kollock's brother, a doctor, in the 1840s. "The cases are also becoming very malignant & do not yield to treatment. I have determined therefore to send my family to [the mountains] immediately."

The disease was all the more terrifying because it was

inexplicable. They did not know that it was carried by mosquitoes. They *did* know that the fever was somehow connected to the nighttime and came to believe that it was caused by the nocturnal exhalation of noxious vapors from decaying vegetable matter. Those who remained in the lowlands in fever time stayed at home when darkness fell, enduring the awful heat with their windows tightly shut against the ubiquitous "miasma." In 1840 delegates to an Episcopal convention in northeastern Georgia found the place to be cool and free of fever. Soon coastal families were building summer houses in the region. They came up in June and stayed until the first frost had eliminated the danger of fever. The lowlanders made the highlands into a place of romance, expressed in the names they bestowed on the region's natural features.

ABOVE: *A copy of Robert E. Lee's farewell address to his army, given after the surrender at Appomattox, hangs over the fireplace in the downstairs bedroom used by Catharine Thoroman's grandmother. She was called "Marmee," after a character in Louisa May Alcott's* Little Women. LEFT: *This deep niche in an upstairs bedroom once held a bed that was used by Kollock children for their afternoon naps. One of the Kollocks remembers scratching animal figures into the delicate blue paint when she was supposed to be napping. The origin of the patchwork quilt has been forgotten.*

ABOVE: *The Gothic Revival style was widely popular in the 1840s, when Woodlands was built. Proponents of the style said that it had a higher moral tone than the "pagan" Greek Revival.* RIGHT: *A print in the dining room memorializes the last meeting of Robert E. Lee and Stonewall Jackson before the latter was fatally wounded at Chancellorsville. The Kollocks were ardent Confederates and placed Civil War prints and other memorabilia around the house after the war. The wicker baby carriage probably dates to the 1880s.* OPPOSITE: *The wardrobe and well-worn rocker in this downstairs bedroom are probably as old as the house and may be older. They may have been among the furniture the family brought up from Savannah when they moved into Woodlands.*

OVERLEAF: *Shafts of winter sunlight pierce a locked gate at one end of the upstairs hall. Kept open in summer, the doorway leads to the roof of the front porch, where one can sit above the veil of wisteria and enjoy a wide mountain view. All the upstairs bedrooms have screen doors. The sounds of one door slamming after the other announced the start of a summer's day.*

Peaks and outcroppings were given such names as Vulcan's Forge, Inspiration Point, Lions' Rock, Devil's Pulpit, Throne of Aeolus, Diana's Rest, and Trysting Rock.

Several decades ago a safe at Woodlands yielded a trove of plantation records and letters describing social life. The family gave masked parties where people dressed as literary characters and did what was unthinkable in Savannah during the fever season—they had nighttime parties outdoors. A letter from the 1840s says that the town "has been very gay this summer, evening parties have been very fashionable every full moon, when the nights were very bright." The letters also provide hints that George Kollock's finances gave him a great deal of trouble. A letter of 1853 from Kollock's sister-in-law says, "I have been thinking much of you &

ABOVE, TOP: *Three stained-glass quatre-foils were set above the main entrance of the house. The amber glass replaced a green pane broken long ago. Catharine believes that the original three colors—red, purple, and green—were put in as religious symbols by George and Susan Kollock, who were devout Episcopalians.* ABOVE, BOTTOM: *Woodlands has several kitchens and dining rooms as a result of shifts in cooking and dining arrangements in the last century and a half. Pots, pans, jugs, and other cooking implements of indeterminate age remain here in the "big kitchen." The blue Dazey Churn has a gear mechanism to ease the task of making butter.* OPPOSITE: *The Gothic Revival bookcases in the library contain books, nature specimens, and memorabilia collected by the Kollocks in the 1800s. The family believes George Kollock designed the cases and that they were built by a local craftsman.*

hope you have succeeded in making some arrangements to relieve yourself of the pressing embarrassments. . . . I do wish you could get into some business in Savannah. . . . Planting is so precarious, for even if you make a good crop you are not sure of selling it for what it is worth."

Kollock was a passionate Confederate. As early as 1851, in a letter complaining about the postal service, he said that such things would be managed better when a "Southern United States" was established. When the Civil War broke out, his three sons, George, Jr., Willie, and Fenwick, left school to join the army. George, Sr., was in Savannah when the city fell to Sherman's army at Christmas, 1864, and barely escaped the Yankees. He fled to Augusta, then to Woodlands, where he took the precaution of burying the family silver, only to have the hiding place discovered by local thieves. The silver was never recovered.

With their slaves freed, the Kollocks were unable to continue raising cotton. They sold their plantation on Ossabaw Island and moved into Woodlands full-time in 1873. George's wife, Susan, opened a boarding school at the house to raise money. The Kollocks' passion for the Confederacy remained hot. To regain his citizenship, the senior Kollock reluctantly took the "Yankee oath" of allegiance to the federal government, remarking afterward, "Bah! Worse than an emetic." Willie joined a Confederate veterans' group and kept a scrapbook with clippings about their doings.

After George's death in 1894 and Susan's in 1896, Woodlands passed to their children. Today George and Susan's great-granddaughter Catharine Thoroman lives behind Woodlands in the old slave quarters, a small house crammed with books, photographs, and scrapbooks. Her cousin John Kollock also lives on the property with his family. The cousins have been deeply influenced by their life in these hills. Catharine is a landscape painter whose work

captures the romantic beauty of this mountainous refuge. John has written several books about the region's history, architecture, and lore, illustrated with his own drawings. Both of them spent summers at Woodlands when they were children, along with many other cousins, aunts, and uncles. John remembers hearing a ghost. "When I was little, and slept in the downstairs bedroom, I used to hear it fairly regularly. It sounded like it had a bad leg, like it was dragging a foot. It was on the second floor, and it would come down the stairs behind my head. I never heard it when I was on the second floor. It usually came in July."

Many years later, as an adult, he experienced other strange sensations in the house when he undertook some slight renovations. "I used to feel presences a lot. I think I

ABOVE: *A Dutch door leads from the big kitchen to the back porch. The top half of the door can be opened for ventilation while the bottom half can remain shut to keep out the dogs.* LEFT: *The big kitchen has a fireplace and two small bread ovens next to it.* OPPOSITE: *In the "big pantry," food was stored in a screened room to protect it from mice.*

119

ABOVE: *Old and new pitchers line the top shelf in a room which the latest generation of Kollocks calls simply "the kitchen." Catharine still refers to it the way her grandmother did, as the "little dining room" or the "children's dining room," because those names are part of the history of the house and she does not want them to be forgotten.* RIGHT: *A pair of old wicker baskets sit atop a screened safe in the house's newest kitchen. Part of the back porch was closed off to make the kitchen, as evidenced by the clapboards behind the safe. Catharine does not call this item a "pie safe," a name she considers a northernism.* OPPOSITE: *A louvered door gives access from the verandah to the library. When George Kollock's sons Willie and Fenwick owned Woodlands and ran its farming operation together, they would come in from the fields to the library whenever an argument arose and smoke their pipes in silence until they were no longer angry at each other.*

was displeasing them for a while, and they made themselves known, I think, because I was disturbing the house. They like it the way it was. There's been a tendency over the years in the family to not want change. I spent a long time, a number of years, painting walls and trying to freshen things up, and the paint's all been thrown back off the walls again. The house has rejected the paint."

Catharine's late husband, who was a professional singer for a time, also felt unseen presences. "He would vocalize in the parlor, and he could feel that there were people around him and that they would guide his music, guide him into what he should do next. I think of them as spirits as opposed to ghosts. Spirits, to me, are helpful, airy, and do pleasant things."

Catharine and John's grandmother, born before the Civil War, spent many summers in the house until 1944. She carried out the routines of daily life just as they had been performed in the 1850s. As John recollects, "Grandmother kept the old, pre–Civil War customs alive until she died, and we grew up that way. She ran the house the way her parents had. It was very, very ordered. The children played on the side porch, never the front porch. We all had to assemble at certain times. Every day we followed the bells—get-up bells, get-ready-to-come-to-breakfast bells, dinner gongs. The servants also ran things the way they had when they were little. Lucy Davis had worked for the family for a long time; Lucy and Grandmother were the same age. Lucy knew exactly what to do. She always dressed formally when we had meals, in a starched apron and a white, flossy cap. By then she was up in her late seventies or eighties. It was run like an old Southern home until Grandmother died in 1944. It was not a matter of Confederate patriotism—it had been a way of life, and it was being remembered. To us it was a living thing."

ABOVE, TOP: *On social occasions the adults gathered for conversation in the library while the children played across the hall in the dining room.* ABOVE, BOTTOM: *This chair, one of Woodlands's few new acquisitions, sits in a dainty little bedroom the owners have always referred to as the "pink room."* OPPOSITE: *The kerosene lamp in the big front room is still in regular use. Only one room on the second floor, the bathroom, is wired for electric lights. Catharine considers this bedroom the nicest because of its spectacular view of the mountains.*

WESTWOOD
UNIONTOWN, ALABAMA

ABOVE: *Westwood is located on a small hill outside of Uniontown. Its tall windows afford excellent ventilation on hot Alabama nights.*
OPPOSITE: *Baby pictures of Ellis Long's cousins Edwin, Willard, and Adele were placed in the house by her grandmother. Attempts to repair the cracked plaster walls were last made in the 1930s.*

*T*he Black Belt of Alabama, named for the darkness of its exceptionally fertile soil, is not picturesque country. This gently rolling crescent of land that crosses the south-central part of the state is given over to agriculture. Huge trucks carrying the products of the land rumble in the heat along Route 80, alongside which tractors gravely patrol the fields. It is a landscape only a farmer could love, but the farmers have loved it dearly for 170 years.

In the three decades before the Civil War, the "flush times," this land produced not only large cotton fortunes but also strange tales. In the 1920s the New York writer Carl Carmer came to the Black Belt to collect stories for his book *Stars Fell on Alabama:* he relates the tale of the planter who dug a hole to hide his silver from the Yankees and unearthed the corpse of his long-lost wife, murdered years before by a former lover; and the story of the handsome doctor who poisoned an invalid and ran off with his wife.

Uniontown, a settlement which occupies the topographical high point of the region, was one of the centers of planter society before the Civil War. It was established in the 1820s by families from Virginia and the Carolinas who,

already well off, came here with their slaves to get rich planting cotton. The work was done in the outlying acres, while the houses that the cotton paid for rose up in Uniontown. There planters spent their money on dinners and dances, showing off the silver ordered from New York, the Brussels carpets, and the French china. It is not so prosperous today.

One of the town's largest houses is Westwood, built between 1836 and 1840 by James Lewis Price, who had come to Uniontown from Virginia. Standing on a hill just outside of town, the house is imposing in its bulk. Two boxy wings, containing bedrooms, extend from the sides of the central block, which holds the formal rooms. It has the simple lines of Greek Revival, without the huge columns sometimes used to signal an owner's status. There is no record of an architect being hired, so perhaps Price designed the place himself with the aid of a guidebook, a common practice in those days. If it lacks the grandeur of the great Southern mansions, Westwood is also free of fussy formality and the relentless urge to impress.

James Price eventually owned forty-seven hundred acres of cotton land around Uniontown. In 1860 one of his daughters, Maria, married Alexander Caldwell Davidson, who bought Westwood as a wedding gift for his bride. Davidson fought in the Civil War, attaining the rank of colonel, and was one of the planters who managed to hold onto their property after the war had freed the work force from slavery. He continued to plant cotton, with paid labor and tenant farmers, supervised the construction of railroads in western Alabama, and served in the state legislature and U.S. House of Representatives. Before and after the war, Westwood was noted for its entertainments. A newspaper account of a daylong dance at Westwood in the 1880s said, "The home of Colonel Davidson is far-famed for its lavish hospitality," and that "a more pleased company never left

ABOVE: *The servants' stairs descend to the back porch where food was once distributed to the plantation's slaves.* OPPOSITE: *Westwood was well known for its entertainments in the late 1800s—"far-famed for its lavish hospitality," in the words of a local newspaper account—and its current occupant, Ellis Long, maintains the tradition. A bit of coconut cake remains on a serving table in the dining room after a party.*

ABOVE: *A large mahogany bed stands in a downstairs bedroom.* RIGHT: *A wide-seated barrel chair, part of a parlor set, was designed to accommodate a lady wearing a hoop skirt. A closet in this room contains a hoop skirt Ellis's mother wore during the round of parties before her wedding in 1938. At that late date, Southern women were still wearing formal dresses that required hoop skirts.*

more hospitable halls. . . . This latest manifestation of the spirit of the old days that is too rarely seen only adds another laurel to their wreath."

The old days continued in the person of the Davidsons' nephew, Louis Davidson, who inherited the plantation. "Uncle Louis," as he was called, was widely regarded as one of Alabama's last survivors of a beloved breed. A 1922 newspaper profile called him a man "of the old South type, with all its rare naiveness and charm." When Carl Carmer came to the Black Belt, Uncle Louis was one of the people he interviewed. A bachelor, Louis had traveled a good deal—Carmer dubbed him the "cosmopolite of the Black Belt"—and entertained the writer with "sophisticated tales of Paris and Vienna and Budapest." Having seen the best that the Conti-

nent had to offer, Uncle Louis told Carmer, "There are only two places in the world where one may live a happy, civilized existence—Paris and Uniontown."

After Uncle Louis's death in 1924, Westwood was inherited by his niece, Adele Ellis Glass, who lived in the house until the late 1960s, when she moved to Texas to join her children and grandchildren. The hospitable halls are now occupied by Glass's granddaughter, Ellis Long, a great-great-granddaughter of the builder. On a visit to Westwood in the 1970s she helped to repair the foundation and dismantled three huge chimneys that were on the verge of collapse: starting on the roof, she removed the chimneys brick by brick, working her way down through the walls. She made another visit in 1985 to repair the plantation's

ABOVE: *A small balcony outside a second-floor bedroom is enclosed by iron grillwork.* LEFT: *A sagging parlor chair, ornamented with a pair of carved acorns, has been relegated to informal duty in a bedroom.*

cotton house, which had been built in the 1870s or 1880s as a residence for the cooks. When she finished the job after several months of work, Long decided to move into Westwood permanently.

When the house had been unoccupied, thieves broke in and stole much of the smaller furniture but could not carry off the massive pieces—four-poster beds, sideboards, and marble-topped dressers. One of the remaining pieces is a huge armoire that had been destined for another house in town but was too large to go through the doors. It fits perfectly in Westwood's stair hall, one of four spacious reception rooms—the others are the parlor, library, and dining room—on the first floor, each averaging four hundred square feet in size, with fourteen-foot-high ceilings that

ABOVE: *This pineapple bed's rich carvings stand out against the window in an upstairs bedroom. The intricate grillwork was placed inside the window lest Westwood's children should fall.* RIGHT: *A small table stands by the main staircase. Visible through the window is grillwork on the verandah, similar to that on the upstairs balconies.* OPPOSITE: *In Ellis's bedroom is a dresser which she used to keep in the offices of a family cotton gin, which she operated with a sister. Ellis sleeps in the "birthing bed," in which three children have been born. Her grandmother had the posts sawn off for unknown reasons.*

retain much of their original decorative plaster. With only the mammoth furniture remaining, the house gives the impression of being lately abandoned by giants, an impression reinforced by the lofty ceilings and floor-to-ceiling windows. On a hot and humid summer night, the air wafts through the immense windows, adding its sighs to the strange mixture of thumps, creaks, rustlings, and slams that sound through any big and aged house when the sun goes down behind the hill.

OAKLAND
BERMUDA, LOUISIANA

ABOVE: *This magnificent bed has always been in the house, as far as Mrs. Prud'homme can remember. She and her husband purchased the dresser when they were married in 1924.* OPPOSITE: *A punkah fan over the dining table displays the family crest. Original to the house, the fan was pulled back and forth by a servant to swish flies from the diners. The sideboard was purchased in France in 1821; the table belonged to Mrs. Prud'homme's mother. The lights were part of an acetylene gas system installed in the early 1900s.*

t was a dark and stormy night when the Lord was mapping off this river, and the only light he had to go by was the lightning, and every time the lightning would flash he would move his pen, you know, move his pen. And the next morning, when he looked at the drawing he had of the river, he said, 'It's too damn much work to straighten it out.' " Alphonse Prud'homme, in his tenth decade, blind and nearly deaf, explains why the Cane River, which passes several dozen yards from his front door, is so insanely crooked. He had heard the story of the Lord and the lightning many years ago from his uncle; but there is no knowing how far back it goes, since Prud'hommes have been trodding these riverbanks since the 1720s. Their plantation is one of only two farms west of the Mississippi that have been in the same family since the Revolution.

Slaves built the plantation house, Oakland, without the aid of any architectural drawings beyond sketches the owner might have drawn up—"I suspect they were just natural carpenters," says Alphonse Prud'homme. The house is one of the simple subtropical cottages whose design was perfected by hundreds of anonymous French and African

builders in the West Indies and along the South's rivers. It is constructed of hand-hewn heart cypress with walls of bousillage, a mixture of mud, Spanish moss, and deer hair. A broad, overhanging roof, like an oversized sun hat, sits atop the one-story building—one story because the French thought a second floor too dangerous in a hurricane. Cottages such as this were decorated sparingly; there is no grand entranceway and no fancy woodwork inside. To raise the living quarters above the damp ground and into the breeze there is a six-foot-high foundation of handmade, sun-dried bricks, which encloses a ground floor that has as many rooms as the living quarters upstairs. Two of these rooms are accessible from above: a wine cellar with a trapdoor to the old butler's pantry off the dining room, and a "Mammy's room" with a trapdoor to the master bedroom, where the small children slept with their parents.

The house is surrounded by a gallery, part of which was enclosed to form a "stranger's room" where wayfarers could stay. The parlor and dining room run through the center of the house, with a large archway between them for ventilation. Flanking these rooms are two sets of bedrooms. Portions of one set of bedrooms were lopped off in the late 1800s to create a narrow hallway.

Oakland is one of several surviving plantation houses on the Cane River, whose banks used to be known as *Côte Joyeuse,* the Joyous Coast. The regular flooding of the Cane made the land exceptionally fertile, supporting a genteel though not highly wealthy society of cotton planters. Their language was French, but their blood was sometimes a mixture of French, Spanish, Native American, and African. The largest town in the region, Natchitoches, started as a fortified French trading post in 1715 and is the oldest permanent European settlement in the territory of the Louisiana Purchase. The first Prud'homme in Louisiana, Jean-Pierre

ABOVE, TOP: *Oakland Plantation had already been operating for decades when the Prud'hommes' cottage was built in 1821. A graceful avenue of oaks leads to the simple plantation house.* ABOVE, BOTTOM: *This doorway originally led from the master bedroom to the verandah. When Alphonse and Lucille Prud'homme took possession of the house in the 1940s they built a dressing room there and replaced the glass panes with mirrors.* OPPOSITE: *The Prud'hommes purchased the red couch in the parlor in 1949, not long after they moved in. Above it is an array of family portraits, including a large one of Ambrose LeComte, the owner of nearby Magnolia Plantation, whose daughter married the first Alphonse Prud'homme.*

ABOVE: *The certificate hanging by the door in the office attests that Alphonse Prud'homme won the gold medal for the high quality of his cotton at the 1904 St. Louis Exposition.* RIGHT: *A portrait of Lise Prud'homme in the parlor of Oakland was jabbed by a saber-wielding Union officer during the Red River Campaign. She and her husband, Phanor, were the second owners of the plantation. Below the portrait is a photograph of a family wedding.*

Philippé, came as a soldier to the fort at Natchitoches in 1720. He stayed on to become a merchant and a trader; his grandson Emmanuel planted indigo, tobacco, and then cotton. (He may have been the first man to successfully plant cotton on a large scale west of the Mississippi.) In 1821 his slaves built the cottage and planted the avenue of live oaks that later gave the place its name.

Lucille Prud'homme tends a thick book of family records and lists of ancestors. She and Alphonse, married for sixty-six years, are the eighth generation of Prud'hommes in America. At Oakland they live among what they call the "new" furniture, purchased in Paris by Emmanuel and his wife in 1821. Other pieces, including a very large full-tester bed, were bought in New Orleans. The "old" furniture

consists of a few eighteenth-century things, including an armoire that Jean-Pierre Philippé brought with him from France. (The original American Prud'homme may have been unusually short, because the armoire has been mounted on eight-inch blocks to make it useful today.) Oakland's antique furniture is of the French colonial type—simple, dark, handsome, and made to last. Alongside it, throughout the house, are modern furnishings, such as a large and striking red couch that stands below one of their oldest family portraits. Walls and tables in every room are covered with the family portraits that chronicle the generations of the Prud'hommes. Emmanuel and his wife, Marie Catherine, had their portraits painted in Paris on their furniture-buying trip; Emmanuel was depicted holding a boll of cotton.

ABOVE: *Mrs. Prud'homme inherited the dresser next to the fireplace in her bedroom from a cousin in St. Louis. The age of the dresser and that of the mirror over the fireplace are not known.* LEFT: *A calendar clock, probably bought in New Orleans, stands on the dining room mantel. The bookcase contains complete sets of the works of Rousseau, Bouffon, Molière, and Voltaire. In the eighteenth and nineteenth centuries many of the Prud'homme boys were sent to France for their schooling.*

A painting of another Prud'homme lady has two saber cuts, inflicted by a Federal officer when General Nathaniel Banks's army passed through in 1864 during the Red River Campaign. In advance of the Union sweep, Confederates had burned the cotton crop to keep it out of Federal hands; then the Union troops confiscated all the food they could carry and destroyed what they could not. Oakland escaped the destruction. According to Alphonse, "The faithful slaves here saved the house—they took all the furniture and everything out of the house, and the Yankees were about to set fire to it, and the slaves asked them not to burn it. And after the war was over, the slaves brought the furniture back." The elderly Prud'homme then residing at Oakland, Phanor Prud'homme, was pulled from the house and forced to march alongside his neighbors to Natchitoches. Too weak to make the journey of several miles, he was left by the side of the road. Some friends found him and carried him to his town house in Natchitoches, where he died.

The passage of the Union army brought an end to the prosperity of the Joyous Coast. Phanor's two sons, who had served in the Confederate army, brought both of their families to live at Oakland to reduce their living expenses while they worked off the plantation's debts. When their finances improved, they divided the property. By the end of the century, the plantation had revived. In 1904, Phanor's son J. A. Prud'homme I won a gold medal at the St. Louis Exposition for the quality of his cotton.

Steamboats were still the chief mode of transporting goods along the Cane in the early part of this century. Alphonse has vivid memories of steamboats arriving at the plantation, slowly threading their way through the river's many turns: "We'd hear the whistle blow and could see the smokestack way down around the bend. We'd run out to the fence to wait for the boat, and we'd have to wait maybe

ABOVE: *A portrait of Mrs. Prud'homme's great-aunt stands next to a bowl and pitcher on a washstand in her bedroom.* OPPOSITE: *The floral quilt at the foot of the bed, made by Mrs. Prud'homme's great-grandmother in 1818, recently won a prize at an exhibition of old quilts in Natchitoches. The flag next to it draped the coffin of a son of the Prud'hommes', who died in 1988. As a World War II veteran he was entitled to a military funeral, at which Mrs. Prud'homme was handed the flag. The bed was made by Prudent Mallard of New Orleans; the armoire with the prominent cornice was purchased in France in 1821.*

an hour before it made all the bends and showed up." He remembers one captain saying that "he'd been up many a river in his boat, but this river was the most crooked river he'd ever been up."

From over 2,000 acres at the beginning of the century, the family's landholdings have dwindled to about 320 acres. Alphonse ran the farm from 1942 to 1962 while also working as the local postmaster. His sons did not fare well when they took over the place: "Things got so bad they went broke; now we rent the property out to someone else." When the Prud'hommes were younger, the house was open to tourists, and they put together an informal museum in the basement. Cabinets and tables display hundreds of items: a Union cannonball fired at the battle of Alexandria, butter churns, baskets, medical equipment (including a hand-cranked machine for giving electric shocks to patients with nervous ailments), rifles, a set of brass knuckles, and a great variety of tools. They have the axes and planes that slaves used to cut and shape the cypress for the house. Two sets of objects reveal that the workaday craftsmanship of Oakland's slaves and free black workers ascended into the realm of art. One is a group of grave markers that were removed from an abandoned black burial ground on the plantation so that the land could be used for a pasture. Only one bears a name, that of the wife of the blacksmith who made the crosses: LAIDE WILLIAMS DIED JAN 21/87 AGE 47. These rusting strips of iron, embellished with simple fleurs-de-lis, once stood in the shadows of cypress trees and Spanish moss next to Bayou Brevelle; even jumbled together against a basement wall, they still have not lost their power as sculpture and as artifacts of faith.

Leaning against another wall is an extraordinary set of wrought-iron well-drilling equipment made by a slave blacksmith named Solomon in the 1820s. According to

ABOVE: Saddles used on the plantation in the 1880s are kept under the porch. Any initials still legible on them probably belong to earlier generations of Prud'hommes. OPPOSITE: For years Mrs. Prud'homme made sausages at this table. The box on the right is a meat grinder; on the left are two sausage stuffers that squeezed the meat into casings. A four-year-old grandson who watched the process declared that he had seen grandmother put hamburger into snakeskins.

family tradition, a French engineer who was acquainted with the Prud'hommes was staying at Oakland when they were planning to dig wells for the plantation. Although the plantation was situated on a river, its water was regarded as impure and was blamed for the frequent bouts of chills, fevers, and other ailments that were actually carried by mosquitoes. It is believed that the engineer made drawings—although none survive—from which Solomon fashioned these exquisite tools. The equipment was buried after the wells were drilled and lay forgotten for a century until it was accidentally discovered in 1924. An expert in petroleum engineering who examined the tools in the 1960s determined that their design is unquestionably French and pronounced them to be the oldest well-drilling equipment in existence anywhere. The equipment was capable of drilling down four hundred feet, driven entirely, of course, by manual labor. The slaves walked in an endless circle, pushing the handles that turned the long rod that twisted the bit deeper and deeper into the earth. Their first three wells came up dry, striking only foul "swamp gas," which is methane. On the next try they hit water.

Several summers ago a young black woman from California turned up at Oakland. She was tracing her ancestors, and the military records of a black Union army soldier led her to his birthplace, Oakland plantation. Mrs. Prud'homme pulled out the plantation's books, where the woman discovered that she was the great-great-granddaughter of Solomon the blacksmith, whose rods, drills, spuds, and augers had brought pure water to Oakland.

ABOVE: *The flower beds in front of the house were laid out in 1835 and later edged with bottles.* OPPOSITE: *Leaning against a wall in the basement is a set of iron grave markers removed from the slaves' burying ground. One of the markers bears the name of the wife of the blacksmith who made them.*

ASHLAND/BELLE HELENE
NEAR GEISMAR, LOUISIANA

ABOVE: *A portrait of John B. Reuss, the great-grandfather of the current owners, hangs in the downstairs hall over a mahogany table from Duncan Kenner's library.* OPPOSITE. *The doors and windows of the second floor open onto a gracious verandah.*

*B*efore the Civil War, the Mississippi River was the boulevard of the newly rich, potentates of cotton and sugarcane whose fortunes ran into the hundreds of thousands of dollars. The River Road, which follows the winding course of the Mississippi, was lined with their mansions. Many of the big houses are now gone, but among the largest and most impressive of the survivors is Ashland, built in 1842 by the sugar planter Duncan Farrar Kenner. Located twenty-five miles south of Baton Rouge and sixty miles from New Orleans, the house stands on a knoll near the river, amid live oaks that were already centuries old when Kenner arrived. Twenty-eight massive square columns surround the house, rising to a heavy Greek Revival entablature and supporting a double gallery. Kenner had its stuccoed walls painted a delicate lemon yellow, making the house a huge bright angular box set down among the dark twisting arms of the oaks.

Duncan Kenner was not yet thirty years old when the house was completed. He had started the plantation when he was twenty-three and had been serving in the state legislature since he was twenty-one. He accumulated his wealth

very fast, perhaps driven by memories of his childhood. His father had been one of the most successful American merchants in French New Orleans until a partner ran off with the company's funds and drove the senior Kenner into bankruptcy. His friends rallied to him, saved what property they could, and paid for young Duncan's education in the United States and Europe. Duncan went to work in the law office of a family friend and took over the remnants of a sugar plantation his father had owned. One of the most valuable assets his father had left him was his network of connections among the Creole business elite of New Orleans. The Creoles cared little for Americans, who flooded into New Orleans after the Louisiana Purchase in 1803, and the Kenners were among the few who were regarded as friends. Even so, Duncan startled both Anglo and Creole society when he proposed marriage to Anne Guillelmine Nanine Bringier, and Nanine startled New Orleans even more by accepting.

Kenner's plantation flourished through the 1840s and 1850s. With his profits he expanded his holdings, on one occasion paying $210,000 for a nearby plantation whose owner, named Trist, did not have Kenner's luck. Trist had built a sugar-processing mill at the cost of $100,000, only to see it burn; its replacement was flattened by a tornado. When he built a third mill, the slaves painted a black stripe of mourning around the chimney; this mill stood, but it bankrupted the unfortunate Mr. Trist.

A burgeoning surplus of funds enabled Kenner to indulge his fancy for horses. He imported thoroughbreds from Europe, built a racetrack around Ashland, and hired a trainer, George Washington Graves, for whom he built a cottage behind Ashland. His horses' red racing colors and his string of successes on the turf gave Kenner the nickname "Red Fox of the South." Gold and silver trophies

ABOVE: *Although the fireplace in this room is actually a plastic movie prop, the real article was originally crafted from black Italian marble. Dinner theater performances, in which pieces of Ashland's furniture are used as scenery, also take place here.* OPPOSITE: *A tall armoire topped by an acanthus leaf is one of the Hayward family pieces brought here from Germania.*

crowded the mantels and paintings of his thoroughbreds lined the walls.

Kenner was one of the most prominent planters in the South when the Civil War began. Elected to the Confederate House of Representatives, he spent the early months of the war in Richmond, leaving his family behind at Ashland. After New Orleans was recaptured by Union forces in 1862, Kenner went home to prepare for the expected Union thrust up the Mississippi by hiding the family silver and the precious portraits of his thoroughbreds. As he was riding to a steamboat landing to receive a shipment of supplies, a slave ran up with the news that the steamboat was not carrying supplies but soldiers. Anticipating just such a surprise raid, Kenner was mounted on one of his racehorses; but the animal, strangely, took it into its head to become stubborn and refused to move. Another planter, in less danger from the Yankees than the Confederate legislator was, gave his horse to Kenner, who galloped past his house without stopping. At the time, his family was sitting on the upper gallery of the house. Hearing the horse pass, Nanine remarked idly, "That man is certainly hurrying," unaware that hoofbeats were the only good-bye her husband had time for. He escaped the Union raiders and returned to Richmond.

The soldiers descended on Ashland, escorted the family to an upstairs bedroom, and searched the house room by room for Kenner. The men were under orders not to damage the house itself or take anything from it. Kenner had hidden his valuables in a slave's cabin, and by some accounts, the soldiers tortured a slave until he told them the hiding place. Either through brute force or diligent searching, the cache of silver and gold was discovered. All was carried off, along with Kenner's fifty racehorses and the plantation's stock of sugar, meat, corn, and other supplies. The soldiers also took a fancy to the horse pictures, which they cut from their

ABOVE: The New Orleans architect James Gallier, Sr., designed Ashland for Duncan Kenner, a wealthy sugar planter. It was renamed Ashland/Belle Helene when the Reuss family acquired it in the 1880s. The Hayward family, its current owners, are Reuss descendants. OPPOSITE, TOP: The sweeping verandah extends the length of the house and provides views of the many live oaks that dot the plantation. OPPOSITE, MIDDLE: A midwinter mist settles over the grounds of Ashland/Belle Helene. The house is only a short walk from the Mississippi River. OPPOSITE, BOTTOM: The urn and pedestal on the verandah were recently acquired at an auction of furnishings from a nearby plantation of the same age as Ashland/Belle Helene. To the right rests an Eastlake side chair.

bulky frames and rolled up. After the Union soldiers left, Nanine and the children packed up what belongings they could and set out for Richmond.

In the last months of the war, the hopes of the Confederacy were pinned partly on Kenner. He had convinced Jefferson Davis that England and France might agree to help the Confederacy if Davis promised to free the slaves. Davis agreed, and dispatched Kenner on the dangerous mission of traveling undercover to New York and thence to Europe. When a friend expressed his anxiety that Kenner might be recognized by one of his many horse-racing acquaintances in the North, Kenner replied, "I'm not afraid of that. There isn't a gambler who knows me who would betray me." The Kenner luck held, as he predicted. He made his way unrecognized to New York, where a hotel manager he had known before the war hid him until his steamship left for Europe. By the time Kenner laid his government's proposals before French and British officials, military events at home had made the offer moot—Lee was trapped by Grant's army outside Richmond, and Sherman was tearing through the heartland of the Confederacy. Kenner was in Paris when the war ended and had to take the oath of allegiance at the U.S. legation in order to regain his citizenship.

The federal government had seized Kenner's lands and turned them over to the Freedman's Bureau for distribution to former slaves. Kenner quickly reversed that action, resumed his business, and saw his financial fortunes soar even higher than they had before the war. His horse-racing days were behind him, but he satisfied his gambler's itch with cards. At his club in New Orleans one evening, he wagered $20,000 and lost. In describing the incident, a historian of the club noted that, since Kenner was one of the wealthiest men in the South, "this was not an unusually large sum for him, and for losing it we would not denominate

him a plunger." He was worth over a million dollars when he died in 1887.

In 1889 Ashland was sold to John Reuss, a Bavarian immigrant who had arrived in the United States as a saddler and ended up a plantation owner. Not long after the purchase, the birth of his granddaughter, Helene, prompted Reuss to rename the plantation Belle Helene. After her marriage to William Hayward in 1908, Helene left the plantation that bore her name. The family removed the furnishings from the house, which has stood empty for most of this century. Vandals broke in and destroyed the only objects of beauty that the family could not take out, the Italian marble fireplaces. When an infestation of the cane borer ruined the fields in the 1920s, the land was subdivided and sold, a bit hastily as it turned out, for Belle Helene was located on an oil field. When the writer Harnett Kane visited the place in the 1940s, oil derricks had sprouted nearby, and the house itself was "empty and forgotten."

Helene Hayward's children have been slowly restoring the house. The cypress floors of the downstairs rooms have collapsed, but the walls and colonnades are still solid, a century and a half after they were erected. Still sturdy as well is the spiral staircase in the hall with its hand-carved walnut rail. Each room on the second story has large jib windows that extend to the floor, allowing access to the breezy upper gallery with its close-up view of the gnarled upper reaches of the live oaks. The Haywards have brought some of the old beds and armoires out of storage to furnish the upstairs rooms. In 1962, a newspaper article quoted the Haywards as predicting that the restoration, with luck, would be finished in two years. The old Kenner luck has not run out, it merely works more slowly than it used to.

ABOVE: *Many of the furnishings in the house, such as this sewing machine from the 1930s, have been brought here from the Haywards' other plantation across the river, Germania.* OPPOSITE: *Duncan Kenner's full-tester bed was made by Prudent Mallard, the noted New Orleans furniture maker. The dresser on the other side of the room has a top of unusual variegated marble. A sculptress who visited the house told the Haywards that marble of this type is produced by only one quarry in Italy.*

ARDOYNE
NEAR HOUMA, LOUISIANA

ABOVE: *Ardoyne is still the center of an active sugar plantation, though its acreage has been greatly reduced. The property is occupied by Margaret Shaffer, the great-granddaughter of the builder, and by her mother. They have preserved the old bell that awakened the workers, summoned them to the fields, and announced mealtimes.* OPPOSITE: *A wardrobe with a mirror and a marble-topped dresser can be found in this second-floor bedroom.*

The plantation house of the Shaffer family, completed in 1900, reveals the festive, romantic, and comfortable character of the Gothic Revival. Its tall, sharp tower soars among live oaks, which surround the house with cool shade, creating the type of picturesque scene that made the Gothic Revival style so popular in the nineteenth century. John and Julia Shaffer were making plans for the house when she became ill and had to seek medical treatment in Paris. Before she left she told John that she saw no need for a big house, and would prefer a small, comfortable cottage. Her health restored, she returned to find work under way on a mansion boasting twenty-one rooms with sixteen-foot ceilings, a sixty-foot-long hall, and a seventy-five-foot tower on the front. John Shaffer's one concession to his wife's wish for something small was the name of the house, Ardoyne, a Scottish word meaning "little knoll."

Located outside the town of Houma, about fifty miles southwest of New Orleans, Ardoyne is in the part of southern Louisiana known as the "Sugar Bowl." John Shaffer's grandfather William came to the region in 1829 from South Carolina to plant sugarcane. At the time Ardoyne was built,

ABOVE: Acetylene lamps were used to light up the outdoors for workers at daybreak. This one hangs on a porch outside the guest bedroom. RIGHT: A sideboard in the hall displays a rare Chitimacha basket, made in Louisiana in the early 1900s, and a hand-made English punch bowl with an intricate floral pattern. Behind the basket is the printing plate that was used to print the checks of Ardoyne's builder.

the Shaffers had nine hundred acres in cane (a modest acreage for the area), a mill, and a six-mile-long railroad to carry harvested cane to the mill. Supplies were brought in by wagon and on paddle-wheeled boats via Little Bayou Black, which runs just across the road from the house.

The house was designed by the New Orleans architectural firm of Williams Brothers and built by the plantation's workers over three years. To provide the building materials, a grove of cypress trees was leveled, shipped to Saint Louis for milling, and shipped back. The architect made the walls out of cypress, rather than less durable plaster, and covered them with wallpaper. The cypress ceilings are coved and crossed with thin beams, providing a hint of a manorial atmosphere without tumbling into pretension.

Indeed, the house has the feel of a pleasant country retreat rather than of a plantation headquarters, even in the long, impressive hall, which culminates in a hand-carved staircase.

Ardoyne's current owner is the builder's great-granddaughter, Margaret Minor Shaffer, who lives there with her mother, Mrs. M. L. Shaffer. Through Mrs. Shaffer's family one of America's most distinguished lineages arrived in this part of Louisiana. They are descended from Nellie Parke Custis Lewis, the step-granddaughter of George Washington. She was the daughter of Martha Custis Washington's son, Jackie, who died of disease during the siege of Yorktown. The Shaffers are doubly descended from the Washingtons, because Nellie married Lawrence Lewis, the son of George Washington's sister, Betty. Mrs. Shaffer inherited several of

ABOVE: *Ardoyne's tower rises seventy-five feet. Completed in 1900, the Gothic Revival house was built by John D. Shaffer while his wife was in Paris for medical treatments. She had told him before she left that she would be happy with a small cottage.* LEFT: *Ms. Shaffer's great-aunt began to collect souvenir spoons around 1915. The Shaffers continue to collect them, and display their finds in racks along the staircase. The house's original wallpaper dates to 1900.*

ABOVE, TOP: *The vanity table in the main bedroom matches the Mallard bed.* ABOVE, BOTTOM: *The Shaffers are descendants of George Washington's wife, Martha Custis Washington, and of the first president's sister, Betty Washington Lewis. A portrait of Washington by Gilbert Stuart hangs in the hall.* RIGHT: *The hall, sixteen feet high and sixty feet long, culminates in an impressive, Eastlake-style staircase.* OPPOSITE: *The crystal is kept in a rosewood chest made in England. Among the Shaffers' collection of china is a set made for Charles M. Conrad, the secretary of war in the administration of Millard Fillmore.*

Washington's personal items, including the first president's watch fob, which she has donated to Mount Vernon. Portraits of the president and of Nellie by Gilbert Stuart, however, remain in the house.

Mrs. Shaffer is also descended from one of the Mississippi Valley's wealthiest cotton- and sugar-planting families, the Minors. Stephen Minor, a Virginian who settled in Natchez, Mississippi, in the late 1700s, was among the richest of the Natchez cotton nabobs. Most of the furnishings in Ardoyne belonged to the Minors and were brought to the house by Mrs. Shaffer when she married Milhado Lee Shaffer, Sr. in 1937.

Her furniture included beds made by Prudent Mallard of New Orleans, a large rosewood breakfront for displaying

crystal, paintings by the great naturalist John James Audubon, porcelain, and a set of china cups made for Charles Montgomery Conrad, the secretary of war under President Millard Fillmore. Among the furnishings of the sitting room are a few accoutrements of Victorian courtship, such as the courting couch, high-backed on the sides and low-backed in the center, to keep a young couple sitting as far apart from each other as possible, and the bronze statuette on the mantel of Cupid stringing his bow. Two antique pianos have not fared well in the humid Louisiana climate; there is an unplayable antique Steinway and another piano that was long ago converted to a desk when its innards rusted away. The oldest piece in the house is an 1808 rolltop desk bearing the label of a Pittsburgh maker. Two large gilded mirrors came from a

ABOVE: *A bathroom was added to the house in the 1920s. Ardoyne was wired for electricity at the same time; previously, it had been lit by an acetylene system. The curved, lidded box on three legs is a baby's bathtub. Mrs. Shaffer bought the tub and the wicker potty at a rummage sale.* LEFT: *Mrs. Shaffer's ancestors, the Minors, collected a large number of clocks. Two of them, a mantel clock and a tall-case clock with three chimes, are kept in this bedroom.* OPPOSITE: *The enormous main bedroom easily accommodates a pair of large half-tester beds and two wardrobes. The nearer bed was made by Prudent Mallard.*

riverboat and a New Orleans hotel, yet they fit comfortably in Ardoyne's spacious rooms.

An octagonal room under the front tower, originally the plantation's office, is crowded with file cabinets and family memorabilia. Among them is a diagram of the World War II battle of Midway and some other naval items owned by Jack Shaffer, a naval academy graduate who survived the Japanese bombing of Pearl Harbor (he was away from his ill-fated ship, the USS *Arizona,* on the morning of December 7) but was later killed when a German submarine attacked his destroyer.

In the 1920s the region was hit with a cane disease—sugarcane mosaic—that nearly wiped out the industry. The Shaffers scrambled to replant their fields with disease-resistant cane from Florida, but had to liquidate their mill and sell their railroad cars and 1897 locomotive to nearby Southdown Plantation. The Minor family also suffered reverses in the 1920s: a bank foreclosed on a loan and took much of their land, just as they were preparing to harvest their crop. A few years later the bank struck oil on the seized property. Next to the house, the Shaffers have preserved a memento of the plantation days: the bell that used to awaken workers at 5:00 A.M. and summon them to the fields at 6:00. Ardoyne is still an active sugar plantation, with 350 acres under cultivation, but the era when every plantation had its own mill and when children could take joyrides on the family's own railroad is gone.

ABOVE, TOP AND BOTTOM: *One of the original acetylene lamps still hangs in the plantation's office, an octagonal room crammed with memorabilia.* OPPOSITE: *A plantation safe once used by the Minors has been converted into a dresser. The small display case on the dresser holds Mrs. Shaffer's thimble collection.*

THE
WEST

THE CHASE RANCH
CIMARRON, NEW MEXICO

ABOVE: *A pitcher in the hallway holds pheasant and turkey feathers. Next to it are an Apache basket made in the early 1900s and a cowbell.* OPPOSITE: *The Chase Ranch was built in 1871 by Manly and Theresa Chase. When they expanded the house in 1879, after the birth of their sixth child, they created this large parlor by breaking through a wall and linking two of the original rooms. The ranch is now owned by their great-granddaughter Gretchen Sammis.*

*L*ong ridges of the Sangre de Cristo Mountains reach out into the grassland plain of northeastern New Mexico, creating a series of beautiful valleys. Walled in by bare, steep-sided mountains, the valleys are broad-mouthed on the east, narrower on the west as the mountains close in. The old ranching town of Cimarron stands in the shadow of the Sangre de Cristos at the beginning of Cimarron Canyon, the pioneers' route across the mountains to Taos and Santa Fe. A branch of the Santa Fe Trail passed through here. Tucked into the valley of Poñil Creek, just north of Cimarron, is the adobe ranch house built by Manly and Theresa Chase in 1871 and owned today by their great-granddaughter. Two stories high, covered with light brown stucco, and shaded by apple trees planted by the Chases in the 1870s, the house is sturdy, plain, and practical, like its builders. It was built in two stages, and on both occasions the builders were in a hurry. What time they had available they spent in making the place solid, not fancy.

When the Chases came to Cimarron in 1867, Manly was twenty-five, Theresa twenty-one. They had already been toughened by life in the West. Theresa had seen her first two

children die in infancy. In his teens Manly had worked as a freighter on the Santa Fe Trail and had barely escaped death on one occasion. At fifteen he was on a wagon train that was attacked by Commanche; only nine of thirty-eight men escaped. Then Manly and his father opened a store in Central City, Colorado, to sell supplies to miners. He met Lucien Maxwell, owner of an 1843 Mexican land grant of 1,714,764 acres in northeastern New Mexico and southeastern Colorado, who had his headquarters in Cimarron. At Maxwell's urging Manly bought a few hundred acres in Vermejo Canyon, built a small cabin, and planted oats, corn, and wheat.

In 1869 the Chases bought another thousand acres from Maxwell, in partial payment for which Manly rounded up about one hundred wild horses and delivered them to Maxwell. In 1871 the Chases moved onto their new property in the Poñil Valley and built a four-room adobe house, which Theresa enlarged in 1879 after the birth of their sixth child. Manly imported fruit trees, to the amusement of his neighbors, who insisted that apples, plums, and pears could not be grown here.

Manly went into the cattle business in 1873 in partnership with John Dawson. For the next two decades Chase rode the economic roller coaster of the Beef Bonanza, wealthy in some years, scrambling for loans in others, always locked in contention with what he called "the growing band of scheming men of the age." Large-scale cattle ranching required huge amounts of capital, which could be obtained only from banks and private investors in the East and Europe. Manly expanded his operations every year through loans from wealthy cousins in New York, Boston, and Vermont and by selling stock to British and Dutch investors. By 1875 Manly and Dawson's company was running one hundred thousand sheep and more than thirty thousand cattle. They expanded further after the Santa Fe

ABOVE: *Manly's daughter, Mary Chase Springer, and her husband, Charles, built a grand set of stone buildings on their ranch, located near the Chase Ranch. This building was their coach house. It was erected in 1904 by Italian stonemasons from stones quarried locally.* OPPOSITE: *Among the family silver is a cream pitcher in the shape of a cow.*

Railroad line reached Las Vegas, New Mexico, allowing them to ship wool, beef, hay, grain, and fruit directly to eastern markets. In 1880 Dawson and Chase took an option on a half million acres of rangeland, and in 1881 Manly founded the Red River Cattle Company with a $500,000 investment from the East, as well as the Cimarron Cattle Company.

In the 1870s and 1880s, Cimarron was one of the wildest of Wild West towns. Its gunmen were not as famous as those of Dodge City or Tombstone, but their victims were no less dead. Most of the fighting erupted over land rights. In 1870 Lucien Maxwell sold his grant to a syndicate of Colorado mining men, the Colorado governor, a judge, and London investors, who organized the Maxwell Land Grant and Railway Company and sold parcels to farmers and

LEFT: *A wood-burning stove made in 1935 is used for cooking and heating. The ranch house does not have a central heating system. A collection of pewter is displayed on a high shelf.* OPPOSITE: *The sideboard and table in the dining room once belonged to Lucien Maxwell, the owner of a huge land grant, who persuaded Manly and Theresa to settle in New Mexico. The Holland Delft china in the cupboard belonged to Lottie Chase, Gretchen's great-aunt.*

ranchers. But squatters were already occupying many choice spots, and more illegal settlers came during the 1870s. While lawyers in Santa Fe and Washington debated the validity of the original Mexican grant to Maxwell's father-in-law, the people of Cimarron shot it out. A minister who preached in favor of the squatters' rights was shot in the back and killed. A neighbor of the Chases, Clay Allison, gathered a vigilante posse that hunted down a suspect and lynched him. When the deputy sheriff, who was the uncle of the hanged man, challenged Allison to fight, Allison coolly suggested that they first have a drink at the local hotel. Standing at the bar, Allison suddenly drew his revolver and shot the deputy dead. Manly was a Westerner of another sort: he firmly opposed violence. He never wore a gun, forbade his men to carry them, and unsuccessfully pushed for laws against cowboys wearing guns on the range.

Despite his murderous encounter with the Commanche on the Santa Fe Trail, Manly was immediately friendly with the Ute and Apache Indians who lived in the mountains around his ranch. There was an Indian agency at Cimarron where food was given out every week. Maxwell had told the Chases to expect the Indians to stop at their place, looking for gifts of milk and bread. The first time the Indians came, Manly greeted them amicably, but Theresa stood nervously at the door of their house with a rifle. Soon the Ute and Apache were coming into the house (they did not feel the need for an invitation) to eat their food in the comfort of the parlor. Afterward they would pull out a pipe for a communal smoke with Manly. The chief of the two tribes, Juan Brailla, began bringing his three children to play with the Chase children and asked Manly to join on a buffalo hunt.

In 1874 hostile Indians came into the area, beat a black worker, and shot arrows at the house. Cheyenne raiders attacked cowboys twelve miles away, wounded Manly's

ABOVE: *An alcove in the parlor holds rocks, Indian artifacts, bullet molds, and natural specimens collected at various times and places. Over it hangs a little cabin, carved for Manly and Theresa by a talented sheepherder, which has appealed to the imaginations of Chase children for decades. They named it "the fairy house." The ceramic figures on the mantel represent Europe and America.* OPPOSITE: *Miniature plates collected by Gretchen's grandmother line the cornice of a cupboard. The clock, made in Connecticut, has been in the house for half a century.*

RIGHT: *A bookcase that belonged to Gretchen's grandmother holds books dating from the 1830s to the 1970s. The set of large red volumes is a copy of the esteemed eleventh edition of the* Encyclopaedia Britannica, *published in 1910, with contributions by Freud and H. G. Wells.*

brother Milt in the head, stole some horses, and killed scores of men. Theresa again began keeping a rifle at hand.

Meanwhile, the Ute and Apache were having their own problems with whites. The Indian agent at Cimarron was corrupt—he gave the Indians rotten meat and pocketed the money he had received for buying good beef. One day in November 1875, Juan Brailla retaliated by throwing a piece of meat in the agent's face and was arrested. Manly, in Santa Fe on business, was unable to help, and on the day after his arrest, Brailla was murdered in jail by his guards. Fearing an Indian attack, Theresa fled from the ranch into town but received a telegram from Manly ordering her to go back. That night Indians who had earlier been guests at the ranch made camp around the house to keep hostiles away. Manly

raced back from Santa Fe and summoned the Indians to his house for a conference with white leaders to defuse the situation. The next morning, at the Indians' request, Manly brought Brailla's body from the jail to the house. The Indians buried him in a cliff crevice near the ranch. No more violence followed, and the Cimarron agency was closed the next year. In 1878 the territorial governor was replaced by the retired Civil War general Lew Wallace, who paid frequent visits to the Chases in the summer. He asked that they not invite any guests to see him because he needed privacy to finish his novel, *Ben Hur*. He wrote in the shade of Manly's apple orchard, sipping Theresa's dandelion wine.

As Manly expanded his ranching operations, he eventually became involved in the management of six cattle com-

LEFT: *Virtually all of the furnishings in the parlor today were owned by Manly and Theresa Chase. The Aubusson rug was spirited out of a mansion in Cimarron one night by Theresa, who took it as payment of an old debt.*

RIGHT: *For several years Theresa urged Manly to expand the house to accommodate their growing family, but he was too busy. When he left for a long business trip in 1879 Theresa summoned the ranch hands and told them to add a second story. Manly was flabbergasted when he returned, but immediately set to work adding even more rooms.*
OPPOSITE: *The front porch looks out upon the apple orchard, where Lew Wallace wrote portions of* Ben Hur. *At the time he was serving as the territorial governor and had become friends with Theresa.*

panies, dealing with a complex network of financial backers in New York, New England, London, and Holland. From time to time, wealthy Europeans traveled to Cimarron to check on their investments. One of them, an Austrian nobleman, had an affair with a young woman, Maybelle Sherwin, who was staying with the Chases. As Manly was sitting in the parlor one night, he heard someone tumble down the steep stairway from the second floor. It was Maybelle, and she was dead; but it was not the fall that had killed her. The Chases found an empty vial of laudanum, an opium derivative, and realized that Maybelle had taken her own life. Their daughter Lottie revealed to them that Maybelle was pregnant by the Austrian, who had promised to marry her and then left town.

Despite Manly's good management and regular infu-

sions of cash from outside investors, the Chase cattle operations began to run into trouble in the 1880s. The range everywhere was overstocked, making it more expensive to feed the cattle just as beef prices were coming down. Several years of dry summers and harsh winters cut into the herds.

Manly himself would have fallen victim to the weather had he not been such a tough character. One autumn Manly, his son, and several men were rounding up cattle when an eight-day blizzard struck. Trapped in a mountain valley, they huddled against the bottom of a cliff to escape the wind. They all would have frozen, but Manly went out into the storm to look for something with which to start a fire. Pawing around in the snow, he found a fallen tree and extracted a rat's nest, which provided the kindling they needed. They had no food until one of their horses froze after standing in the snow for two days.

Theresa had her own brush with death. On a late spring afternoon, she was walking near the ranch when a wildcat sprang on her from a tree. As the cat tore at her face and arms, Theresa locked her hands around the animal's throat and kept squeezing until it fell unconscious. Then she smashed its head with a rock. Her life had been saved by her amazing strength and by her corset, which protected her chest from the animal's claws.

The Chases faced their worst crisis in the early 1890s, when a national financial panic caused banks to fail. Burdened with debt, the Chases decided to sell the ranch in 1894 but could find no takers. They managed to ride out the financial storm, however, until cattle prices rose in the late 1890s. Theresa Chase died in 1900, and Manly turned the day-to-day running of the ranch over to his sons, Mason and Stanley. He spent his own time tending to his fruit orchards until he died in 1915.

After Stanley's death in 1954, his granddaughter

ABOVE: *Gretchen sleeps in the room and in the bed where she was born. The cherrywood bedroom suite was carried by oxcart over the Santa Fe Trail from Missouri when Manly and Theresa came out to New Mexico.*

Gretchen Sammis bought out the other heirs and operated the ranch while also working as a teacher. Since 1963 Ruby Gobble has been forewoman of the ranch. A national roping champion for four consecutive years in the 1950s, Gobble first came to the ranch when she needed pasture land for her own herd of mares. Sammis and Gobble oversee eleven thousand acres, a relatively small spread in the Southwest, where some ranches extend for hundreds of thousands of acres. At roundup times when extra help is needed, Sammis calls upon a group of women friends to become cowgirls for a few days. The cattle are no longer driven to railheads—huge trucks now come to the ranch to pick them up. One of the problems of the old days, rustlers, still lingers. In one recent cattle roundup, Sammis came up short of her expected count and suspected that someone "borrowed" a few head.

Except for the addition of a metal roof, the ranch house has not significantly changed. Most of its furnishings date to the 1880s: handsome leather-covered chairs, an Aubusson carpet, fine bedroom sets and cabinets, paintings and prints of hunting scenes, and an ample stock of books. Some of the furniture is older; it was hauled by oxen over the Santa Fe Trail. Old rifles, saddles, and spurs hang on the wall in the cluttered ranch office. The expensive imported carpet came to the house in an odd way: when a friend was fired from the presidency of the Maxwell Land Grant Company and lost his company-provided mansion, he invited Theresa to sneak into his former home with him by night and take out anything she liked, in payment of a debt he owed the Chases. She chose the carpet.

Just a few steps from the house is the family cemetery. The first person to be buried there was the Chases' daughter Lottie, who died in 1893 several months after giving birth. She lies near her parents, the rancher who refused to use a gun and the woman who could strangle a wildcat.

ABOVE: *In Gretchen's office at the ranch house are spurs going back to the 1870s, a turn-of-the-century sidesaddle used by Mary Chase Springer, and three rifles. The one in the middle is a combination of rifle and double-barreled shotgun made in Prussia, with beautifully engraved damask steel barrels.*

BLUMENSCHEIN HOUSE
TAOS, NEW MEXICO

ABOVE: *An artist from Taos Pueblo, Telesfor Romero, made this carved stone head and gave it to the Blumenscheins in the 1930s.* OPPOSITE: *In 1919, Mary and Ernest Blumenschein purchased several rooms in one the oldest adobes in Taos. A late painting by Ernest Blumenschein, "Arizona Landscape," is on the easel in his studio. The needlepoint cushion on the stool was made at Taos Pueblo. Blumenschein seldom used the portable paint set; he did most of his painting in the studio rather than outdoors. In the early 1920s this was the place where Taos artists had their dance parties because it was the only room in town with a hardwood floor.*

In the early summer of 1898, a twenty-four-year-old artist named Ernest Blumenschein was riding painfully on horseback down a mountain pass in northern New Mexico—painfully, because he was holding under one arm a broken surrey wheel, giving him muscle cramps. He was on his way into the nearest town, Taos, to get the wheel fixed, having left his friend Bert Phillips back in the mountains with the surrey. The two were heading for Mexico to find exotic landscapes to sketch, but the landscape Blumenschein saw on the Taos road told him that he need go no farther. The ride was, he said, "twenty slow miles of thrilling sensation." Describing it years later, he was still so overwhelmed that he could not write an entirely coherent sentence: "The sky was clear, clean blue with sharp moving clouds, the color the effective character of the landscape, the drama of the vast spaces, the superb beauty and serenity of the hills stirred me deeply. . . . New Mexico had gripped me." He retrieved Phillips, and the two "pitched into work with unknown enthusiasm." Blumenschein spent the next few months in Taos, then went back East, where he had commercial assignments awaiting him.

For Blumenschein and the other artists who followed him, Taos, its landscape, and its people were exactly the type of "exotic" subjects that Gauguin had traveled half the world to find. Taos is one of the oldest settlements in America. Tiwa Indians had been living in the area as early as A.D. 900. The Spanish established a mission there in 1598, and one hundred years later Taos started becoming an important trading center. Taos Pueblo, a complex of four- and five-story adobe buildings, is still a thriving community whose artists are famous for their textiles and pottery. The adobe architecture of the pueblo, which the Spanish adapted for their settlement, was one of the subjects that caught Blumenschein's eye. Made of mud bricks and covered with a smooth coating of stucco, the houses seem to spring directly from

LEFT: *The spare bed in the dining room is one of the most important pieces in the house. Of a type known as the Taos bed, it was made in the 1930s by a Spanish craftsman working under the auspices of the WPA. During the Depression the WPA sponsored programs in different parts of the country to encourage the preservation of regional art and crafts, which were in danger of dying out.* OPPOSITE: *Mary furnished a corner of the library with an armoire and chairs which she and her husband had bought in Paris when they were art students.*

RIGHT: *The paintings in the dining room, collected by Ernest Blumenschein, are part of a remarkable group of works done in the 1920s and 1930s by Indian artists who were using European media for the first time. The narrow shelf, which runs around the perimeter of the room, displays a wide array of ceramics, metalwork, and basketry. The dining room is in the oldest part of the house. Its beamed ceiling dates to the 1780s. Above the beams and the split cedar shakes is a layer of dirt that serves as insulation.*

the soil, having the color and age and regenerative power of earth. Adobe houses are rarely torn down; they are renewed, patched, added onto—a centuries-long collaboration of one generation after another. In 1919 Blumenschein and his wife, the painter Mary Shepard Greene, bought four rooms in one of the town's newer adobes, a single-story building dating to the 1780s that stretches along the old southern wall of the town. The previous owner of the rooms was a painter from Maine, Herbert "Buck" Dunton.

Born in Pittsburgh, Blumenschein had grown up in Dayton, Ohio, where he went to high school with one of the Wright brothers and the man who invented the cash register. He had originally wanted to be a musician (Dvořák chose him as first violinist for an orchestra he was assembling in New

York) but switched to painting. Before and after his visit to Taos, he studied art in New York and Paris and quickly found success as an illustrator of magazines and books. He illustrated works by Jack London, Stephen Crane, Hamlin Garland, Willa Cather, Joseph Conrad, and Booth Tarkington. Putting pictures among the words of great writers paid well but did not provide him with a great deal of satisfaction. He yearned to be a real painter, and Taos was the place, he thought, where he would find the light, colors, and subjects to become one. In 1910, more than a decade after his first visit to Taos, he began spending his summers there. Two years later he helped organize the Taos Society of Artists, whose other founding members were Bert Phillips, Oscar Berninghaus, Irving Couse, Buck Dunton, Kenneth Adams, Walter Ufer, Victor Higgins, and Joseph Sharp.

The merchants of Taos saw the benefits of having a community of artists in their midst—painters attract tourists. Storekeepers were generous with credit to the artists, sometimes accepting paintings in lieu of cash to settle accounts. The Atchison, Topeka & Santa Fe Railroad was also eager to promote travel to the area. One of its officials, W. H. Simpson, realized the public-relations potential of paintings of the Southwestern landscape and gave free passes to painters. The railroad purchased numerous paintings, hung them in stations in the Midwest, and used them in calendars, brochures, and on posters. Railroad officials were not the most sensitive art patrons, as one painter discovered when he was told, "We want a Taos Indian group subject, full of sunshine and smack." On the other hand, some of the Taos painters were not unwilling to turn out canvases that would sell quickly. Photographs of the society show a group of neatly groomed, dark-suited men who could be taken for accountants. Blumenschein was pleased that their work was helping to make New Mexico a popular

ABOVE: *Helen Blumenschein decorated the dining room door with brass studs and a medallion which her mother had collected. The small woven basket with a lid, on the shelf to the left of the door, is a rare Chitimacha basket from Louisiana.*

OVERLEAF: *On a bedroom wall, behind a Philco radio, Mary hung a linen tapestry which her husband had purchased in Germany in the early 1900s when he was an art student.*

tourist destination, but he was quick to denounce Irving Couse for what he thought was out-and-out commercialism. Couse's painting of an Indian squatting in front of a buffalo hide won a national competition for a calendar image, and Blumenschein said Couse had been painting that same squatting Indian ever since.

Perhaps the most intellectual of the Taos painters, and a bit stiff-necked, more than once Blumenschein alienated his fellow painters with his loudly stated opinions. During World War I, he published an article questioning his colleagues' patriotism because they refused to paint targets for the army's artillery practice. At an angry society meeting, the members forced him to print an apology. Disputes were to be expected among a group of artists living in close proximity, all painting the same landscape and the same Indians, and all aware of who was making money and who was not. In a moment of what must have been exquisite agony, Blumenschein was at the post office when another painter, Victor Higgins, opened a letter containing a $10,000 check.

Taos presented Blumenschein with "whole paintings right before my eyes. Everywhere I looked I saw paintings perfectly organized, ready for paint." During his long career in Taos, between 1910 and 1954, he painted from four hundred to five hundred canvases: portraits of Indians at the pueblo, of Hispanic townspeople, landscapes, scenes of Indian festivals, even the plasterer who came to fix his house. Within a few years after his return to Taos in 1910, his work gained international recognition. He had two pictures, *Wise Man, Warrior and Youth* and *Peace Maker*, on display at the Pan Pacific Exposition in 1914; one of them won the silver medal. At a Chicago Art Institute exhibition in 1917, he won a gold medal and $1,000 for *The Chief*. In his paintings he accentuated the bright colors of clothing, making them stand out against tawny backgrounds of adobe.

ABOVE AND OPPOSITE: *The Blumenscheins did not have a kitchen until the late 1920s, and the house wasn't electrified until the 1930s. The portrait over the refrigerator depicts Emilia Montoya, who worked for the family as a cook. It was done by Helen Blumenschein.*

He was borrowing from the vivid palette of the fauvists, whose work he had seen in Paris, trying not to distort reality but to capture it, as anyone who had felt the lustrous force of the New Mexican sun would know.

Blumenschein's work did take a toll on his family life. For years his wife and daughter, Helen, stayed in New York, which offered urban conveniences and a sophisticated social scene that were missing from Taos. When he talked Mary into making a visit, she left immediately upon finding that she would have to care for Helen in a boardinghouse. The housing problem was solved in 1919 when Mary sold a brownstone in Brooklyn that she had inherited from her parents and bought Buck Dunton's four rooms in the old adobe. As adjacent occupants died or moved out, the

RIGHT: *In the 1940s, the Blumenscheins purchased an electric stove, which can also burn wood.*

Blumenscheins expanded their residence by knocking a hole in a wall to make a doorway, until they eventually had twelve rooms, plus a screened-in room on the roof where Helen could sleep outside in the summer.

The Blumenscheins' set of rooms roughly forms a T, with a courtyard on the left side of the house. The top of the T represents the rear wall, overlooking the Rio de Don Fernando, where Indian women once washed their clothes. The stem of the T contains an entry room, the kitchen (installed in the late 1920s and early 1930s), and the dining room. The kitchen is long and narrow, but the dining room is spacious, with a ceiling of split cedar strips. The largest room in the house is the studio, about twice the size of the other rooms, with a double-height ceiling and large windows. The

LEFT: *At the end of the long and narrow kitchen are small shelves, built by Mary throughout the house to display collections of arts and crafts.*

familiar geometry of the conventional American dwelling place is absent from this rambling set of rooms. Like all adobes it is a place of irregular rectangles with odd, soft corners and sloping ceilings; no line is straight and no edge sharp, as if the world has gone slightly out of focus.

Mary happily immersed herself in the task of decorating the house. In a memoir of her family's life in Taos, Helen Blumenschein described how her mother "did a beautiful job of keeping the original simplicity and form of the rooms." She added windows that were horizontal rather than vertical, which was the traditional form, but she kept the Indian fireplaces and Spanish woodwork. She put up shelves to display ceramics and hung Japanese prints in the library and Southwest Indian watercolors in the white-washed dining room. Under Mary's direction a local craftsman painted the walls of the library with a hand-mixed Venetian red color. Mary herself painted some decorative motifs on a wall and designed a piece of furniture that was made for her by an Indian carpenter. She mingled locally made furniture with furniture she and her husband had bought in France when they were art students. To preserve the simple, pre-mechanical spirit of the home Mary built a mock fireplace to hide a water heater.

In her memoir Helen wrote that decorating the home in Taos unleashed her mother's pent-up talent for design. Helen said that with some paint her mother could make a Montgomery Ward bed and chair "look as though they had come from fairyland." She made party dresses by hand and began fashioning silver jewelry. In the early 1920s Mary gave up her career as a painter, a career that had shown a great deal of promise. She had won prizes in Paris for her paintings in 1900 and 1902, a silver medal at the 1904 St. Louis Exposition, and the 1915 Julia Shaw Prize of the National Academy of Design. Taking care of her young daughter took time away from her painting, but it was also said that she gave up painting because her husband could not stand having two painters in the house. With her eye on a new career as a designer, and her daughter's well-being also in mind, Mary took Helen back to Brooklyn for a few years so that she could study jewelry design and Helen could attend a good preparatory school. Helen decided not to attend college and instead embarked on a career as an artist, a decision that caused her parents some uneasiness, "as they knew the pitfalls," Helen said.

Mary and Helen rejoined Blumenschein later in the 1920s, when the Taos art colony was entering its heyday. "Taos is now a whirlpool of self-expression," wrote a journalist, as the town saw an influx of new artists and writers, many of them from Europe. D. H. Lawrence took up residence outside of town with his wife, Frieda, at the invitation of the wealthy patroness Mabel Dodge Luhan, who had left her second husband to marry a Taos Indian. Marsden Hartley was in town and doing some of his finest work. Georgia O'Keeffe arrived in 1929.

The 1920s were the last decade of the old ways in Taos. Electricity, telephones, and indoor plumbing were just over the horizon. Helen Blumenschein remembered the church bell that woke everyone at 6:30; the smell of piñon smoke hanging over the town from heating and cooking fires; the bitter winter cold and the fresh summer vegetables delivered from a ranch by buggy; the wagon that brought springwater; the fishing trips into canyons; the mountainside hunting expeditions for deer and turkey; and the weekly bowl of rabbit stew. The rhythm of artistic inspiration was set partly by the rhythm of life at the pueblo, where the seasons were marked by dances and festivals. Blumenschein and the other artists attended and painted the two springtime Corn Dances, the Deer Dance, the New Year's Day Turtle

ABOVE: *By the bedroom fireplace is an antique box which the Blumenscheins acquired in Taos. Spanish in design, it was probably made about 1850 but could be slightly older.*

Dance, and the Buffalo Dance, which was also performed in the midwinter chill of January to the accompaniment of a "chorus of blanketed Indians with a fine deep resonant drum," as Helen wrote.

In the 1940s, when Blumenschein's health began to fail, he painted fewer pictures than before but gathered in a harvest of honors. The University of New Mexico bestowed an honorary degree; the Museum of New Mexico mounted a retrospective exhibit. Collectors bought all of his major paintings, some of which had sat for decades, unwanted, in the studio. Many of his canvases went to the Gilcrease Museum in Tulsa, Oklahoma, and the Stark Museum in Orange, Texas, two major museums of Western art. By the 1950s the mountain winters became too much for his health. He spent the cold months in California or Albuquerque, where he painted one of his best works, *Railway Yard—Meeting Called,* which hangs today in the studio. He died in 1960, about two years after his wife.

Helen maintained the house in the 1950s and 1960s, and rented out the rooms for a time in the 1970s. She later put her family's possessions back and deeded the property to the Kit Carson Historic Museums, which opened the home to the public, as Helen wished. The house is furnished as it was when the Blumenscheins lived there, with their books, the Indian art they collected, and works by other painters who experienced the "thrilling sensation" of the Taos landscape. "We lived only to paint," as Blumenschein wrote in an essay looking back on the heyday of the art colony, "and that is what happened to every artist who passed this way."

ABOVE: *Taos Indians traditionally painted doors and windows blue because that color was believed to ward off evil spirits.*
OPPOSITE: *An Indian from Taos Pueblo made the chair for the Blumenscheins out of willow branches. Willow was an important symbol in the iconography of the Taos Indians, who called themselves the Red Willow People. Ernest Blumenschein painted the trout on the door to celebrate his biggest catch.*

RIORDAN HOUSE
FLAGSTAFF, ARIZONA

In the 1880s three Irish brothers from Chicago, sons of an immigrant carpenter, came out to the rough-and-tumble lumber mills in the Arizona Territory and made a fortune. Denis Riordan was the first. After failing to strike it rich in the goldfields of California, he took the job of Navaho Indian agent at Fort Defiance in Arizona. He met the territorial governor, who introduced him to a Flagstaff mill owner, who gave Denis a job. He was soon running the mill and took it over when the original owner decided to sell out. In the mid-1880s Denis invited his brothers Tim and Michael to join him in Flagstaff. The three Riordans ran the mill together until 1894, when Denis decided to spend some time traveling. He sold the company to the younger Riordans, who named it the Arizona Lumber and Timber Company.

The two Irish-Catholic brothers married two German-Catholic sisters, Caroline and Elizabeth Metz. Tim and Michael decided to build a single large house for their two families—each would have a wing, with a large common room in the middle. In 1903 they hired the architect of the company whose purchases had made their mill prosperous, the Atchison, Topeka & Santa Fe Railroad, and built the house out of

their own fine product, virgin pine logs. No French châteaux were dismantled to build the place, no palazzi stripped of their tapestries and statues to furnish it, yet there are few American houses of the late Gilded Age that breathe a greater sense of self-confidence, properly moderated pride, and pure happiness than does the rustic mansion of the Riordans.

The two brothers had opposite temperaments. At six feet two inches and two hundred pounds, Tim was a giant in those days, the good-natured boss who could get a full day's work out of a hard-bitten gang of loggers. It was said that while traveling in Spain, he was mistaken for the king of Sweden and ushered into a royal reception. He was called by his initials, T.A., and by the nickname "Ya-Ya," due to his habit of bellowing "Yi! Ya!" to announce his arrival when he came

home at night. He loved jokes, the outdoors, and sports. He had a clay tennis court built on the grounds and a "nine-hole" golf course—there were only three holes, but each had three approaches. When his company dammed a stream to create an artificial lake (which he named Lake Mary after one of his daughters), Tim immediately saw the recreational possibilities. He ordered a motor launch and a sailboat, *Illini*, which was the first sailing craft to ply Arizona waters since the days of Spanish exploration in the sixteenth century.

In a family photograph taken in Chicago, Michael is several inches taller than Tim, but Tim is sitting down. Michael always wanted to be a Jesuit priest; indeed he was in a seminary when Denis invited him to come west and he decided to go because the dry air would be good for his

ABOVE: *Tiffany & Company made the ceiling fixtures and a set of stained-glass windows, with a tulip motif. The tulip windows on Michael's side have a blue background.* LEFT: *Among the items that were left behind in Michael's wing of the house when his daughter Blanche gave the property to the state of Arizona were a straw basket, arrowheads, and a bow. The Riordans helped finance John Wesley Powell's archaeological digs at Walnut Creek Canyon, not far from Flagstaff.*

tuberculosis. A studious man, he kept the mill company's books as secretary-treasurer. His hobby was collecting exotic woods from around the world (Tim collected rocks). He helped to establish the first Catholic church and the first library in Flagstaff. Both brothers were highly devout Catholics. In each wing of the house, there is an informal chapel, a large landing off the main stairway where the families prayed every day. Both brothers made pilgrimages to Rome, and Timothy had audiences with three popes.

Their house stands atop a knoll, now covered with trees, that once commanded a sweeping view of Flagstaff. The grounds extended for fifty acres. Altogether the house has forty rooms and thirteen thousand square feet of living space. The architect, Charles Whittlesey, designed the house in the Craftsman style—spacious, informal, and comfortable. Much of the furniture was made by Gustave Stickley and Harvey Ellis, two masters of the Craftsman style. The house was up to date in its conveniences, with central heating, hot and cold running water (the Riordans liked to show guests the bathrooms), and electric lights. The Riordans later installed the first telephones in Flagstaff. (The town had only four phones at the start—in the mill, the railroad station, and in each of the Riordan wings; they were all party lines.) Stained-glass tulip windows, chandeliers, and lamps were ordered from Tiffany and Company, and in the conservatory, also used as a breakfast room, Tim installed a small fountain.

The Riordans' common room is almost nine hundred square feet in size. On opposite sides of the room they kept a billiard table and a piano, reflecting masculine and feminine pursuits. By the fireplace rests a pair of huge shoes, almost two feet long, fashioned from bark. Timothy made them, telling his daughters that they were Paul Bunyan's baby shoes. For some of the windows, Michael ordered "window transparencies," large black-and-white photographs on

ABOVE: *Very devout Catholics, the Riordan families each had a chapel and prayed together every day. The statue of Christ was imported from Italy. After her sudden death from polio in 1927 Anna Riordan was laid out here.* OPPOSITE: *The fireplace in Michael's wing features an inglenook, an enclosure that formed a cozy fireside sitting area.*

glass of Indian chiefs, Indian ruins, and natural wonders of the Southwest. They were made by Jack Hillers, the great frontier photographer who went on John Wesley Powell's second exploring expedition through the Grand Canyon. The Riordans were fascinated by the Indian culture of the Southwest and often made trips by wagon, and later by automobile, to visit ruins and see the Hopi snake dances.

The two Riordan wives did their best to create a proper household. Caroline was small (about five feet tall, eighty-five pounds) but commanding. She disapproved of Tim's smoking, limited it to one room, and insisted that he burn incense when he smoked. Both mothers were strict with their daughters (Tim and Caroline had two daughters; Michael and Elizabeth had two daughters and three sons).

ABOVE: *One of the Riordans bought a stuffed golden eagle for the common room in the 1930s. The purchaser was most likely Tim, as Michael was opposed to hunting. In the 1930s there were no restrictions on the hunting of eagles, which were still common in Arizona at the time.* LEFT: *Elizabeth Riordan commissioned Louis Akin to paint a Ponderosa pine, the source of the family's milling fortune. Framed in bark, it stands on a wall of the common room.* OPPOSITE: *The common room at the center of the house was often called the billiards room. With its bare wooden walls and ceiling of peeled log beams joined with wooden pegs, the room epitomizes the rustic style, yet harmonizes perfectly with the Craftsman style of the other rooms in this rambling house.*

ABOVE: *All the fixtures in the kitchen on Timothy Riordan's side of the house are original. It has a coal-fired stove that was used until 1977.* RIGHT: *After the Riordan house was acquired by the state of Arizona the rooms on Timothy's side of the house were cleaned and brought back to their appearance in the early 1900s, using only items that had been found in the house. The rooms on Michael's side were left as they were, reflecting seven decades of use by different members of the family.*

Tim's daughter Anna was in the mold of her father: she was a sportswoman, traveled around the world with her father, wore "daring" sleeveless dresses, and annoyed her mother by wearing pants when she went riding. On the other side of the house, Elizabeth intoned "a lady never leans back" as she instructed her girls in the correct manner of sitting on the edge of a chair, knees and ankles together, hands folded on lap.

The unusual pattern of siblings marrying siblings was nearly duplicated by the next generation of Riordans. Tim's daughter Mary and Michael's daughter Blanche married two brothers, Bob and Walter Chambers. The marriages were advantageous to the senior Riordans because the father of the Chambers brothers was a vice-president of the Santa Fe

Railroad, whose freight rates partly determined the profits of the Riordan mill. Elizabeth also made use of this alliance. When she needed servants for a party, she wired the Santa Fe office in Chicago requesting that Pullman porters be let off the train in Flagstaff for a night.

As a business team, the brothers meshed well, with Tim as the go-getting head of the company and Michael as the methodical administrator. Even their different political affiliations—Michael was a Republican; Tim, a Democrat—may have been part of a plan to straddle the political fence. For over forty years, the siblings maintained their amicable, mutually profitable partnership. Closely linked in so many ways, the brothers also shared a tragic coincidence in 1927. During a picnic in September, Anna Riordan complained of headaches and difficulty breathing. The next day she was paralyzed from the waist down and was diagnosed with polio. Michael's son Arthur came down with the same symptoms and within hours both of them were unable to breathe. The families desperately tried to keep Anna and Arthur alive through artificial respiration as a special Santa Fe train raced from Chicago to Flagstaff carrying an iron lung. It arrived too late; the cousins died on the same morning—Anna at age twenty-six, Arthur at thirty.

After Michael died in 1930, Timothy decided to sell the mill because no one in the family was interested in taking on the business. Caroline died in 1943, Tim in 1946, and Elizabeth in 1954. The last member of the family to occupy the house was Blanche, who died in 1986, bequeathing the house and many of the family's furnishings and effects to the state of Arizona. From time to time, Blanche smelled the scent of burning tobacco and found ashes scattered about when no smokers had been in the house; and recently some have heard, echoing from the common room, a faint clicking of billiard balls.

ABOVE: *The window transparencies of Indian chiefs and landscapes in the common room were made by the renowned western photographer Jack Hillers, who accompanied John Wesley Powell on his second exploration of the Grand Canyon.*

RANCHO SAN JULIAN
LOMPOC, CALIFORNIA

Rancho San Julian encompasses some thirteen thousand acres in southwestern Santa Barbara County, south of Lompoc and not far from where Point Conception juts out into the Pacific, at the juncture of the Santa Ynez Mountains and Santa Rosa Hills. Coastal fogs roll through the rugged hills, covered with live oaks and chaparral, and through the San Julian Valley where cattle and sheep graze. Since the 1830s this land has been in the de la Guerra, Dibblee, and Poett families, three lineages that converge in the current proprietor, A. Dibblee Poett, known as Dibbs. He is thin and craggy-faced, with hands his nephew compares to gnarled oak.

The Casa San Julian, or ranch house, is a sprawling adobe filled with furniture used by five generations of Dibbs's family. The earliest pieces were made in Spain and in Spanish colonies such as Peru, Chile, and Mexico; when California was under Spanish dominion, the authorities would not permit furniture to be imported from anywhere else. Beyond offering this basic identification, Dibbs has only a vague idea of the origins of various pieces and their stylistic names. His interests do not particularly run to things that are indoors;

but in matters of dirt, plants, the tricks of the cattle trade, the shifting winds at dusk, the weight of a cow's footfall, and the way that frost turns the sweet-tasting Sudan grass into a cud of cyanide, his knowledge is encyclopedic.

The first of Dibbs's ancestors to hold this land was José de la Guerra, who was named comandante of the Santa Barbara presidio in 1815. At his suggestion the authorities set aside forty-eight thousand acres as a government ranch to supply beef and grain to the presidio. When de la Guerra was granted personal ownership of the ranch in 1837, he built a bedroom and a *sala,* or living room, in what is now the west wing of the house. Dibbs believes that de la Guerra built upon the foundations of an even older structure, a simple adobe hut built around 1805 by a priest and a soldier who often traveled this way en route to Mission La Purísima Concepción in the Lompoc Valley. De la Guerra's sons added bedrooms, a dining room, and a large kitchen that prepared food for the ranch hands. A later owner built the east wing in 1878. A large porch on the eastern side of the house catches the morning sun and offers a protected place to sit in the fall when the harsh westerly winds blow.

For four decades de la Guerra successfully managed a ranching and trading empire that stretched for a hundred miles along the California coast. He was shrewd enough, and tough enough, to survive the transitions from Spanish to Mexican to American rule. His sons were not so canny. They enjoyed living well, borrowed more than they should have when times were bad, and lost their father's huge ranch piece by piece to creditors in the 1860s. In 1867, two of the men who acquired Rancho San Julian, which was just one portion of the original de la Guerra holdings, were Albert and Thomas Dibblee, whose family had one of the oldest European lineages in America. The first Dibblee settled in Dorchester, Massachusetts, in 1636.

ABOVE, TOP: *Until 1925 the gilt mirror in the drawing room remained in the house in Santa Barbara where Thomas Dibblee lived before he married Francisca de la Guerra. The old Dibblee house was destroyed in the 1925 earthquake, but the mirror was salvaged from the ruins and brought to the ranch. Dibblee Poett cut it in half so that it would fit over the fireplace; the other half is used in another room.* ABOVE, BOTTOM: *A piano is one of two musical instruments in the drawing room. There is also an old serafina much prized by the family. When an earthquake struck the area in 1925 Francisca Dibblee cried out, "Save the serafina!"* OPPOSITE: *Many of the books at Casa San Julian belonged to Henry Dibblee, the youngest of the three Dibblee brothers.*

ABOVE: *Quica Mia, a devout Catholic who ate fish every Friday even though it sometimes made her ill, set up this devotional niche with a statue of a saint flanked by candles.* RIGHT AND OPPOSITE: *Francisca Dibblee, who married Thomas Dibblee in the late 1860s, was called Quica Mia, "Dearest One," by her grandchildren. Although she died in 1932, at the age of seventy-four, her bedroom is still known as Quica Mia's room. In the middle of the summer she would come out from Santa Barbara for a stay at the ranch. Dibblee Poett remembers that his grandmother "generally came . . . with her two unmarried daughters . . . laden with enough trunks, boxes, and suitcases for an extended stay abroad." It was a family joke that some of the luggage was never even opened.*

Albert Dibblee came out to California for his health in 1848 and made a fortune selling supplies to the gold rush miners. He bought a 15,600-acre ranch in 1858, raised sheep for the wool market, and went into the dynamite business. Rancho San Julian and other lands were purchased later by Dibblee in partnership with his brother Thomas and Colonel W. W. Hollister. The de la Guerra line was returned to San Julian when Thomas married José's granddaughter, Francisca de la Guerra.

The Dibblee-Hollister partnership ran what may have been the largest sheep-raising operation in California. When competition from New Zealand and Australia made the wool business less profitable in the 1870s and 1880s, the partnership increased the size of its cattle herds. The ranch

flourished, raising cattle, sheep, and a variety of foods—such a variety that the operation became virtually self-sufficient. There was enough homegrown food to feed the owners' families, the crew, and a small horde of hangers-on. Workmen, passing wagon drivers, cowboys, and tramps all timed their travels so that evening would bring them to the gate of Rancho San Julian, where they could get supper, a spot in the barn to sleep in, and breakfast.

Albert and Thomas Dibblee both died in 1895. Thomas's widow inherited Casa San Julian and about four thousand acres. Other property was divided up among Thomas's children. In 1891 Alfred Poett was hired to survey the ranch and brought his son Fred along to hold the chains that marked off the acreage. The job took so long, four and a half years, that there was ample time for a romance to flame up between Fred and Mercedes Dibblee, the daughter of Francisca and Thomas. According to a story Dibbs was told, Fred had to compete for Mercedes's attentions with an Italian count. The two suitors decided to settle their conflict with a horse race through the streets of Santa Barbara, which Fred won. He and Mercedes were married in 1902, and Dibbs was born four years later.

Dibbs, who has written a book about the history of San Julian, has a rich store of memories of life in these hills. His earliest recollection is from 1910, when he was taken outside at the age of three to see Halley's comet streaking across a quarter of the sky. His boyhood on the ranch, which was managed for many years by his uncle Wilson Dibblee, was filled with the adventures that city kids dream about. He and his sisters often rode on the wagon that delivered the ranch's bean crop to the mill in Lompoc, where the driver would treat them to a package of Nabisco cookies. On the return trip, they would curl up on the empty burlap bean sacks in the back of the wagon and go to sleep. Their nap

was always interrupted when the wagon passed beneath a particular oak tree, from which hung a swinging tin sign—when the wind swayed the sign, it made a ghostly metallic sound that never failed to frighten the children.

Dibbs's childhood companions were sheepherders and vaqueros. The vaqueros talked to the cattle, and the sheepherders talked to themselves, a habit they fell into at their remote camps, where each herder spent many weeks away from all human contact. One of the ranch's sheepherders, Alfredo Espinosa, carried on two-sided conversations with himself which he accompanied with a grand display of hand gestures. Alfredo performed a variety of tasks at the ranch, including gardening, keeping the stables, cooking, and predicting the weather. He could sense the approach of heavy rain by the progress of his friend Pico's rheumatism. "Pico has rheumatism in the left leg," he would say. "When he gets it in the right leg it will rain like hell." San Julian's blacksmith had the job of mixing poisons with molasses and barley to eradicate squirrels. He tested the strength of the mixture by taking a little nibble himself and developed an immunity to arsenic and strychnine.

Cattle drives to the railroad were the highlights of the ranch calendar. Uncle Wilson and a half dozen cowboys would take Dibbs along on the short drive to the railroad siding. They would be up at five in the morning to coax a half-mile-long string of cattle down a dusty road, up and down steep hills, through a canyon, and past a blacksmith shop that was a local gossip exchange. The hardest labor of the drive took place at the railroad siding. After the cattle were loaded onto a car, the cowboys had to move it with muscle power and large crowbars, then roll up an empty car. Later in the day, a freight train would stop to pick up the cars. The last of these drives took place in the 1930s; after that, trucks began to come to the ranch to pick up the herds.

ABOVE: *The tendril of a grapevine has begun to enfold a wicker bench on the porch.*

From working at the side of Uncle Wilson, Dibbs learned the secrets of the grasses (which ones can withstand heavy grazing in a dry season and which cannot); the psychology of the weigh-in at a cattle sale (always get to the scale before the buyer); and the two methods, neither of them pleasant, for relieving cattle dangerously bloated with gas. In the 1930s Dibbs was given the job of managing part of Rancho San Julian, and when Wilson died in 1951, he took over management of the entire operation. By that time the ranch received a steady income from the earth itself. Some of the San Julian lands consist of diatomaceous earth—deposits of fossilized diatoms that were formed on an ancient seabed that was uplifted to form the California coast. This porous material makes an excellent filter for

ABOVE: *For over a century the de la Guerra, Dibblee, and Poett families have gathered under a grape arbor for barbecues.*
LEFT: *The tranquility of the ranch is broken from time to time by the thunderous sound of a rocket lifting off from Vandenberg Air Force Base, which is adjacent to Rancho San Julian.*

chemical processes (it was initially used for filtering beer). A succession of firms have quarried this earth from Rancho San Julian since the 1940s.

In 1969 Dibbs and his aunts decided to sell their cattle, lease some rangeland to other ranchers, and set up a trust to ensure that the land would be passed on to future generations of the family. In the 1930s the Poetts and Dibblees had turned down an offer of $1,000,000 for Rancho San Julian from Will Rogers. The cowboy humorist instead bought a neighboring spread, which eventually became the Vandenberg Air Force Base. Every now and then, the San Julian Valley shakes with the force of a small quake as a rocket blasts off. Dibbs was relieved when the government decided not to

ABOVE: *The furniture in Mercedes Poett's bedroom came from the Thomas Dibblee house, which was destroyed in the 1925 earthquake.* LEFT: *A worn horsehair chair from the de la Guerra era is still used in this bedroom.* OPPOSITE: *A portrait of Frederica Poett and her chow dog by Cecil Davis hangs in the bedroom used by Frederica's mother, Mercedes. The portrait was done in the late 1930s or early 1940s.*

base the space shuttle at Vandenberg—the launches might have shaken the ranch house to pieces.

On his side of the fence, Dibbs continues his resolutely earthbound pursuits, dispensing advice to his nephew James Poett, who is now raising cattle on the ranch. James has learned to interpret the sometimes cryptic utterances that emanate from a man who has spent a lifetime observing nature's minutiae and has found that the most important matters are the most basic ones. Dibbs once started a discussion about moving cattle off drought-weakened rangeland simply by grabbing a fistful of dirt and asking, "Why does the grass grow?"

RIGHT: *The enclosed porch is furnished with a cushioned bench in the Craftsman style.* OPPOSITE: *Casa San Julian lies in a valley among the Santa Ynez Mountains and Santa Rosa Hills. The hills abound in wild strawberries and blackberries.*

ROBINSON HOUSE
BEVERLY HILLS, CALIFORNIA

Harry and Virginia Robinson were the pioneer homesteaders of Beverly Hills. Driving around Los Angeles one night in 1908, looking for a newly opened country club, they got lost in a remote part of town. Near a hilltop at the end of a road, Harry Robinson climbed out of his car, took a look around, and declared to Virginia that this was where they would live. It was a bold decision because Beverly Hills was then a virtually empty, bare patch of hills where lima beans had once grown and where a hunt for oil had recently failed. The oilmen, to recoup their losses, named the area after the upper-crust resort town of Beverly Farms, Massachusetts, and divided it up for development. The only structure in the district, as Virginia later recalled, was "just a little bit of a real estate office, kind of a shed." The next morning Harry made a visit to the man in the shed and bought just over six acres of land around the hilltop he had chanced upon in the dark. Virginia's father, the architect Nathaniel Dryden, agreed to design their house.

If Harry had bought more of those bare acres, he could have reaped a huge fortune, but speculation was apparently not on his mind. At any rate, the young Robinsons did not

need the money. Harry's father was the founder of the J. W. Robinson department store chain; Virginia's father was also wealthy, being the owner of a large ranch in Texas. When the Drydens came out to Los Angeles in the 1880s, Nathaniel could not find proper rooms for the family to stay in, so he rented an entire boardinghouse for a few months. One of Virginia's earliest memories is of having five dollars in her pocket and spending it all on handkerchiefs. Recalling that purchase in an interview with the writer Walter Wagner more than ninety years later, she made no bones about it: "I was a spoiled child."

The residence Nathaniel Dryden built for his daughter and son-in-law is not as grand as some of the mansions that later sprouted around it. Being pioneers, the Robinsons had

ABOVE: *In 1913 Harry and Virginia Robinson built the first mansion in Beverly Hills, a Beaux-Arts house designed for them by Virginia's father, Nathaniel Dryden. His only other building in California is an Islamic-style library in Glendale, now used as the Brand Library.* LEFT: *The walls of this second-floor room in the pool house were painted to simulate blocks of marble. Some of Virginia's books stand on a French chest inlaid with metal and mica.* OPPOSITE: *Pompeiian art was the inspiration for the pool house murals, done in a style called grotesque.*

ABOVE, TOP: *The drawing room in the main house features a gilded French console table, backed with mirrors, displaying animal figurines and a French Baroque clock. Most of the furniture has been in the house since it was built.* ABOVE, BOTTOM: *Attached to a large mirror, the portrait of Virginia Robinson seems to float in the air over her morning room, where she received guests during the day. The furnishings are early-twentieth-century reproductions in the Louis XV style.* OPPOSITE: *The fireplace in the morning room was made of Carrara marble. Flanking the French clock are portraits of Virginia's family; in the oval frame to the left of the clock is a portrait of Virginia as a young girl.*

no standard of magnificence to go by, no neighbors to over-shadow. Completed in 1913, the house is a single-story, six-thousand-square-foot stucco building in the Beaux-Arts style. Of architectural interest is the two-story pool house, designed by William Richards and completed in 1924. It has a stronger classical theme than the main house, with a portico featuring Tuscan columns, long, low balustrades, and large square windows that make it a sunny place. The light is further enhanced by lattice-covered mirrors on the first floor.

As soon as the main house was finished, the Robinsons gave a party. If the guests found the place a bit remote, their notions of social geography would be forever changed a few years later when Mary Pickford and Douglas Fairbanks, Sr., moved into a nearby hunting lodge and rebuilt it into a mansion the press called Pickfair. Beverly Hills was launched. Pickford, who became Virginia's lifelong friend, helped her in an awkward social situation early in her career as a hostess. Virginia liked to see her lawn full of people having fun, even if she did not know them. At one of her huge parties, to which Virginia had invited Hollywood people whom she had never met, Pickford came over and said, "Goodness, this is disgraceful. No one has the slightest idea who you are." A bit shy and easily lost in a crowd ("a little button of a woman," said one reporter), Virginia was about to retreat inside. But Pickford took charge: she had a butler bring two chairs and told him, "We will sit here, and everybody is to be introduced to us." Since no one would dare snub Mary Pickford, Virginia Robinson was thus introduced to Hollywood society.

Entertaining became one of Virginia's two chief pursuits; the other was gardening, which she undertook with seriousness and success. Advised by the landscape architect Charles Gibbs Adams, she transformed her six acres into a lush landscape of exotic trees, shrubs, and flowers, including the Jamaican earpod, the Guatemalan devil's hand, and

ABOVE: *The loggia on the east side of the house looks out over an Italianate balustrade to the palm collection in Virginia's extensive gardens.* RIGHT: *The architect of the pool house, William Dodd, included Palladian mirrors as part of his classical revival scheme for the building. The removal of paint put on in the 1950s has revealed the ceiling's original decoration—whimsical scenes of birds, cats, dogs, and other animals.*

a white-flowered hibiscus from the Hawaiian island of Kauai. She took full advantage of the hilltop setting, carving out terraces for thematic plantings, patios for resting and reading, and a network of winding paths. She had irrigation and drainage systems installed, as well as fountains and pools. On the eastern slope, she planted an impressive grove of king palms, native to the eastern shore of Australia. On the cool northern slope, she placed an aviary amid a woodland. Fragrant camellias, gardenias, and citrus trees were arranged on the southern exposure. Her one failure, oddly enough, was an attempt to plant persimmons, pomegranates, and olive trees, which thrive elsewhere in California. She replaced these with two dense acres of ferns and palms. At various places she planted rows of eucalyptus and cypress trees.

To maintain her garden, she kept a staff of twelve full-time gardeners; and to populate it she kept a troop of monkeys. Her husband bought their first monkey from a pet shop that was not taking proper care of it. He had noticed that it was being kept in a sunny window, paid the shopkeepers to move the animal to a shady spot, paid them more to feed it correctly, visited the monkey every day to check on its care, and finally decided that the simplest thing was to take it home. The monkey seemed lonely, so the Robinsons acquired a mate; soon they had a family of monkeys. The animals had the run of the garden until too many overly friendly guests were bitten; then the animals were caged.

In the 1930s, 1940s, and 1950s, Virginia's pool house was one of the centers of Beverly Hills and Hollywood

ABOVE AND LEFT: *A spiral staircase ascends to the second floor of the pool house. The second floor was the site of Virginia's bridge parties, attended by some of Hollywood's most famous stars, including Eddie Cantor and Fred Astaire. Cantor, she said, "was a great player."*

society. Harry Robinson died in 1932, and while she mourned his passing for quite some time, she continued to give an August Moon party to celebrate her birthday, and benefit parties to support the musical programs at the Hollywood Bowl. Her guests included Ethel Barrymore, Irene Dunne, Loretta Young, and Sir Anthony Eden. Fred Astaire and Eddie Cantor came to play bridge. Her largesse extended to her pets: she let her monkeys drink Champagne, but not the dogs—the dogs got candy. She fed dinner promptly at 4:30 to all the neighborhood cats every day. Her own two cats lived on the roof, to which she built a special stairway just for them. In recognition of her social achievements, she was named first lady of Beverly Hills in 1964 by official proclamation.

In a place where the most devoutly desired miracle was perpetual youth, it could not escape notice that somehow Virginia Robinson thrived decade after decade as so many of her guests went down before the scythe. Doctors came and asked about her secrets. She swam and played tennis until she was in her mid-eighties; she danced until she was in her nineties (giving it up when the Simon and Garfunkel song "Mrs. Robinson" became popular—orchestras were always playing it and everyone would stop dancing and stare at her); she was never far from a small glass of Champagne. It was her custom to have ninety people for lunch every Wednesday by the pool, at tables set up on Persian carpets to protect the grass. She maintained this custom despite the fact that her staff was not as large as it once was. "I'm down to just the six servants now," she told an interviewer in 1975, when she was ninety-seven. She missed living a full century only by a few weeks.

ABOVE: *A single place setting of Dresden china is always on display in the dining room. Virginia was served all her meals here when she was dining alone.* OPPOSITE: *The Robinsons' guest book is kept on a console table in the main entrance hall of the mansion. A mirror has been removed from the niche for restoration.*

ENNIS-BROWN HOUSE
LOS ANGELES, CALIFORNIA

ABOVE: *A bronze panel depicting the Mayan god of fire overlooks the dining room. Although Wright was clearly influenced by Mayan architecture when he designed the house, he never alluded to any such influence in his writings.* OPPOSITE: *A small table and chair have been placed on a mezzanine overlooking the dining room.*

ntil 1968 August Brown was living what he calls "a very staid existence" as an administrator of employee benefit plans. Brown and his wife were shopping for a house in the Los Angeles area without luck when their real estate agent, having exhausted his listings, tentatively suggested a 1920s Frank Lloyd Wright house in pitiful condition. The huge house stood brooding at the top of a hill, with long, bastionlike retaining walls, a set of terraces, and a forthright, truncated tower that calls to mind a Mayan temple. It had been occupied by a gun shop owner who neglected to maintain the place, used only a couple of rooms, and displayed a banner-sized FOR SALE sign that was visible for miles. The pipes were so deteriorated that there was no longer any hot water in the kitchen. Despite the decay Brown was immediately taken with the house and made the purchase that changed his life into something that has been "tremendous, wonderful, most pleasant." In addition to playing host to Wright devotees from around the world, he has met Hollywood stars, directors, and producers because the house has been repeatedly chosen as a movie set. But Brown loves the place itself more than the glamour

that has descended upon it: "I appreciate every part of it. Every room has so much meaning. It's a house of surprises."

Wright built the house in 1923 and 1924 for a wealthy clothing merchant, Charles Ennis, and his wife, who made a bit of a nuisance of herself during construction. Wright's son Lloyd was supervising the work and wanted to ban her from the site, but his father wrote from his headquarters at Taliesin that Mrs. Ennis had "the right spirit," and that "to stave her off would only arouse her suspicions and be bad for the result." Later, after the Ennises had quarreled with Wright and installed iron decorations and marble floors which the architect detested, he referred to them as "ignorant fools." Charles Ennis had a measure of revenge on the master. Either by his own choice or by that of his friends, Ennis's funeral was held in the house, conducted by the Order of Knights Templar, the highest-degree Masons of the York rite, with pomp and rituals about which one can only speculate. That event began the house's long association with the macabre. While no ghosts are known to walk its long terraces, the house gained local notoriety in 1958 when it was the setting for a popular horror movie with Vincent Price, *The House on Haunted Hill.* For years after, it was the custom of teenagers to test their nerve by trying to get into the house. The first nights Brown and his wife spent there were interrupted by the clamor from dozens of teenagers who ran onto the grounds screaming. The Browns put up signs and handed out leaflets explaining that Vincent Price did not live there, that the house was a great architectural landmark, and that the new owners were perfectly normal people who wanted to sleep in peace. A columnist from the *Los Angeles Times* wrote about their plight, and the nocturnal visits came to a halt. This first experience, however, did not deter Brown from renting out the house for other action and horror movies, such as *The Annihilator* and *The Howling II.* The

ABOVE, TOP: *Charles Ennis commissioned Frank Lloyd Wright to design a house for him in the early 1920s. When the Ennises complained about cost and schedule over-runs, Wright soothed them with a vision of the future: "the final result is going to stand on that hill a hundred years or more."*
ABOVE, BOTTOM: *The Ennises added wrought-iron embellishments to the entranceway.* OPPOSITE: *Wright referred to the loggia, living room, and dining room as "The Great Room" because of the free flow of space among the three areas.*

OVERLEAF: *When John Nesbitt was the owner in the early 1940s he and Wright discussed a renovation of the house. The outbreak of World War II put an end to the project. The only change that was completed was the addition of a pool, which has a view of the Santa Monica Mountains.*

ABOVE: *The guest bathroom has its original green tiles. The Mexican painted chair was purchased by Augustus Brown. The window overlooks the valley.* RIGHT: *An antique adding machine which Brown acquired is kept in the kitchen pantry. The linoleum was installed by Brown.*

director Ridley Scott also used the house with great effect in *Blade Runner* and as the residence of a sinister Japanese gangster in *Black Rain.*

The house was one of Wright's California "romanzas," a term he borrowed from music. As he wrote in his autobiography, he took the term to denote "freedom to make one's own form." In designing his California houses, he said that he took inspiration from musical forms: "A musician's sense of proportion is all that governs him in the musical romanza: the mysterious remaining just haunting enough in a whole so organic as to lose all evidence of how it was made." The house is just as Wright describes—a mystery governed by a sometimes elusive sense of proportion. It is an interplay of geometries, of concrete in harsh and gentle aspects, of colors

both blunt and soft. It was built of plain and patterned concrete blocks cast from decomposed granite quarried at the site. The patterned blocks are used as a decorative element and to impart a rich texture to what could have been a severely geometric interior. Wright was enthusiastic about the architectural qualities of concrete; he wrote in his autobiography: "We would take the despised outcast of the building industry—the concrete block—out from underfoot in the gutter—find a hitherto unsuspected soul in it—make it live as a thing of beauty—textured like the trees. . . . Outside— well, in that clear sunshine, even the eucalyptus tree would respect the house and love it for what it was."

Wright said that the sense of space is what architecture is all about, and the Ennis-Brown house is an essay on

ABOVE, TOP AND BOTTOM: *The bathroom of the study features marble walls and sink and a stained-glass window over the bath.* LEFT: *Wright did not often devote a great deal of attention to kitchens, but designed an ample one in the Ennis-Brown House. Many of the appliances were in place when Brown purchased the house, although he does not know if they are original.*

manipulating space. Massive from a distance, the house seems even more so when it is approached; but entering the house is an intimate act on a smaller scale. The entrance is not set into the forbidding walls but is located off a protected courtyard. The visitor ascends a stairway into a broad room gently lit through stained-glass panels—one of the surprises August Brown finds most pleasing.

In 1940 the house was purchased by a movie producer named John B. Nesbitt, who sent a letter to Wright relating how he had become immediately enchanted by the house: "After one casual visit I was unable to sleep for three nights. I saw at once that its plan was precisely matched with my habit of life." He was writing to the architect to obtain the blueprints to start repairs on an alarming one-hundred-foot-long bulge in a retaining wall. Without seeing the house, Wright dismissed Nesbitt's fears: "No need to worry about the slight bulge." Nesbitt, like Mrs. Ennis, seemed to have the right spirit. The new owner and the architect carried on a jocular correspondence. The outbreak of World War II, however, ended plans for a restoration (or "resurrection," as Wright called it) of the Ennis House and for a new seaside house Nesbitt had commissioned. After Nesbitt sold the house in 1942 it passed through several owners until August Brown took possession. Although he resides in the house he has opened it to the public, by appointment. In doing so, Brown has helped to fulfill a prediction which Wright made to the Ennises when he was trying to soothe their worries over costs and schedules: "Long after we are all gone it will be pointed out as the Ennis House and pilgrimages will be made to it by lovers of the beautiful—from everywhere."

ABOVE: *The circular patterns of a wire bench, purchased by Brown, make a pleasing contrast with the Wright's angular geometric designs.* OPPOSITE: *The stunning patterns of Wright's concrete block construction also embellish the walls of the master bedroom.*

Design by Diana M. Jones

The text, set in ITC Berkeley Book and Bernhard Cursive Bold,
was composed with QuarkXpress 3.0 on a Macintosh IIsi and
output on a Linotronic L300 at The Sarabande Press,
New York, New York.

The book was printed and bound by
Toppan Printing Company, Ltd., Tokyo, Japan.